nifty**notes**

on
Jennifer Johnston's
How Many Miles to Babylon?

by
Aoife O'Driscoll

FOR LEAVING CERTIFICATE
ORDINARY AND HIGHER LEVEL

educate.ie

PUBLISHED BY:
Educate.ie
Walsh Educational Books Ltd
Castleisland, Co. Kerry, Ireland
www.educate.ie

EDITOR:
Adam Brophy

DESIGN:
The Design Gang, Tralee

PRINTED AND BOUND BY:
Walsh Colour Print, Castleisland

IMAGES –
WWI photos on pages 11, 13, 33, 45; Frank Hurley (1885-1962), official photographer to the Australian Imperial Forces, courtesy of the Imperial War Museum, London. Recruitment poster page 26: Library of Congress Prints and Photographs Division, Washington, D.C.

The author and publisher have made every effort to trace all copyright holders. If any have been overlooked we would be happy to make the necessary arrangements at the first opportunity.

ISBN: 978-1-908507-38-9

Acknowledgements

I would like to thank everyone at Educate.ie for their help and support, particularly Adam Brophy for his wonderfully constructive advice, patience and encouragement during the writing process. I would also like to thank Naomi Kloss for her insightful and helpful suggestions, and the design team for creating such a visually pleasing book.

Dedication

This book is dedicated to my mother, Neans, the best teacher I have ever known, and to my beloved sister, Ciara.

Aoife O'Driscoll

CONTENTS

Futility

Move him into the sun—
Gently its touch awoke him once,
At home, whispering of fields unsown.
Always it awoke him, even in France,
Until this morning and this snow.
If anything might rouse him now
The kind old sun will know.
Think how it wakes the seeds –
Woke, once, the clays of a cold star.
Are limbs so dear-achieved, are sides
Full-nerved, – still warm, – too hard to stir?
Was it for this the clay grew tall?
– O what made fatuous sunbeams toil
To break earth's sleep at all?

Wilfred Owen
1893-1918
English poet and WWI soldier

INTRODUCTION

Whether you are studying *How Many Miles to Babylon?* as a Single Text or as part of your Comparative Study, you will find notes to help you in this book.

Here you will find a detailed summary and analysis of the plot, as well as in-depth character sketches, notes on each of the comparative modes for Ordinary Level and Higher Level, and a step-by-step guide (including sample answers) on how to approach this novel as a Single Text.

How many miles to Babylon?
Three-score and ten.
Can I get there by candle-light?
Yes, there and back again.
If your heels are nimble and light,
You will get there by candle-light

~ Anon

the scoop

Title

How Many Miles to Babylon? is a children's nursery rhyme

Setting

Wicklow, Ireland, and then Flanders, Belgium

Time

Prior to and during World War I

Plot summary

The story is narrated by Alec Moore, an Anglo-Irish officer in the British army. He is in a military prison in Flanders and is facing execution. As he waits, he looks back over his life to date and reflects on the events that have led him to his present situation.

Young Alec grows up in a large house in County Wicklow, the son of wealthy, Protestant Anglo-Irish parents. His parents' marriage is a deeply dysfunctional one and Alec, an only child, is lonely and unhappy until he strikes up a secret friendship with Jerry Crowe, a local peasant boy. Alec's mother comes to hear of the friendship and orders Alec to stop seeing Jerry.

War breaks out and Alec's mother insists that he join the army so that she can be the mother of a hero. Jerry also joins the army and the pair remain friends. Their superior officer, Major

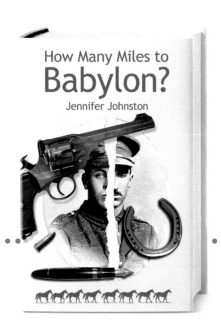

How Many Miles to
Babylon?
Jennifer Johnston

Glendinning, disapproves of the friendship as Alec is an officer while Jerry is only an enlisted man.

Jerry receives a letter from his mother, telling him that his father is missing in action. Major Glendinning refuses to allow Jerry to go and search for his father so Jerry goes absent without leave. Several days later, he returns, having found out that his father is dead. Jerry is arrested, charged as a deserter and sentenced to death by firing squad. Major Glendinning orders Alec to command the firing squad. Alec cannot bear to do this so he visits Jerry in prison and shoots him dead in order to spare Jerry the agonising wait. In turn, Alec is arrested and is sentenced to death himself. The novel ends where it began, with Alec in prison, calmly waiting for his execution.

Themes

The novel centres on the friendship between Jerry and Alec. It also explores the way in which Alec is emotionally damaged by his largely loveless upbringing and by his parents' dysfunctional marriage. Other themes include class distinction; Alec's attempt to escape his miserable life and to find happiness with his friend; and the horror, futility and despair he discovers in the trenches of World War I.

Historical background, summary and analysis

1

Home Rule in Ireland at the outbreak of World War I

John Redmond was the leader of the Home Rule Party from 1900 until his death in 1918. This political party wanted to gain self-governance for Ireland but did not want Ireland to be independent of Britain, nor did it support the use of violence to achieve its aims.

The Home Rule Party was opposed by different groups in Ireland. The Ulster Volunteers were formed in 1913 with the express aim of stopping the introduction of Home Rule, using arms if neccessary. This

John Redmond

threat was met by the formation of the Irish National Volunteers in the south of Ireland. The Irish National Volunteers comprised different groups, some of which supported Home Rule and some of which were in favour of using force to achieve Irish independence. These latter groups did not believe that Home Rule went far enough.

The Home Rule Bill was passed on the 18th September 1914 but it was decided that it would not come into force until the war was over. Two days after the passing of the Bill, John Redmond called on the Irish National Volunteers to join the British army and fight in the war. He believed that this would help the Home Rule Bill to gain popularity in Britain. At the same time, the Ulster Volunteers called on their men to join up in order to show their loyalty to Britain. Over 200,000 Irish men fought in WWI. In the south of Ireland the Anglo-Irish supported the union with Britain and the war effort, while nationalists joined the army at the urging of John Redmond or simply for economic reasons. The Irish National Volunteers split on the issue. Some continued to support Redmond, but others did not want to fight for Britain and did not believe that doing so would further the cause of Irish independence.

One of Redmond's opponents was Padraig Pearse. He had

supported Home Rule at first but increasingly came to believe that Ireland would never gain independence from Britain while so many people in Ulster opposed it. When war broke out in 1914, Pearse saw an opportunity for Irish rebellion while the British were busy fighting the Germans. He became one of the leaders of a group which split from Redmond and began to prepare for insurrection.

Life in the trenches

Dangers

Life in the trenches was extremely dangerous, not just for the obvious reasons of attacks, shellfire and enemy snipers, but also because of the constant threat of disease. Rats, lice and fleas were ever present, as were the decomposing corpses of dead soldiers. Between 125,000 and 166,000 men from the Allied Forces were killed, wounded or declared missing in action at the First Battle of Ypres in 1914.

The reality of daily life in the trenches

Discomfort

It was not just the danger and disease that made life in the trenches so miserable; it was also the discomfort. The soldiers suffered from cold, dirt, waterlogged conditions, filth, and lack of sleep. Men had to stand guard for hours on end and if they fell asleep the penalty was death by firing squad.

Attempts were made to ensure that each man on sentry duty was regularly relieved and allowed sufficient time to sleep but the reality was that night-time attacks and alarms were so frequent that it was difficult to get a few hours of unbroken rest.

The stench of filthy soldiers, rotting flesh, unsanitary latrines, dead rats, lime and mustard gas was constant and it made visitors to the front recoil in horror. But soldiers became almost used to the appalling smell.

The Cycle

Jennifer Johnston's account of the trench cycle is an accurate one. Each battalion would typically spend some time in the front line, followed by several days in the support trenches and then a few days of rest in a reasonably safe location before going back to the front line again.

The penalty for a soldier found guilty of dereliction of duty was usually death by firing squad

Daily Routine

Day began at dawn, with 'Stand To'. All men had to be at their posts, ready and waiting for a possible enemy attack. Stand To lasted for about one hour, after which the men would have breakfast. There was often an unofficial ceasefire between the British and the Germans at this time to allow the men on both sides to have a meal in relative peace. However, senior officers frowned on such practices and if they came to hear of such a truce, soon put an end to it.

After Stand To, the men who were not on sentry duty tried to catch

some sleep. Men in the reserve trenches brought supplies to the soldiers in the front line trenches. Senior officers occasionally patrolled the trenches and carried out inspections.

Patrol inspecting the trenches

At nightfall, the dawn routine was repeated and soldiers were placed on alert. If there was no attack, the men were permitted to 'Stand Down'. However, as the risk of attack increased during the hours of darkness, sentry duty was doubled. Work on the trenches was carried out at night, particularly in those areas that might be more vulnerable to enemy fire in daylight. If relief was to be provided and troops replaced, this was generally done during the hours of darkness.

Some soldiers were sent forward to repair or build up the wire in No Man's Land (the area between the opposing armies' trenches). Others were sent to listen at enemy posts in order to gain intelligence. If enemy soldiers encountered one another in No Man's Land, they had a choice: they could engage in hand-to-hand fighting or walk away. Using guns in No Man's Land was too risky as it exposed the fighters to enemy fire. In *How Many Miles to Babylon?* Major Glendinning uses a knife to finish off a wounded soldier from the Gloucestershire Regiment because to use a gun would signal his location to the Germans.

Flanders, Belgium 1915

The narrator, Alec Moore, sits in a military prison in Belgium, awaiting his execution. As he is 'an officer and a gentleman', he is allowed pen and paper with which to record his thoughts. He seems oddly unmoved at the thought of his impending death, and claims that he feels this way as he does not care about any cause, nor love any living person. It seems that he has nothing to live for. He has decided not to write to

his parents, instead leaving it to the British army to inform them of his death after the event. The news, he feels, may kill his father but that might be a mercy. He says that his mother's reaction is of no interest to him.

He has not been visited by Major Glendinning, and is glad of that. As we do not yet know who the major is, we wonder why Alec should not want to see him. The military chaplain has visited several times, but his attempts to offer comfort and to persuade Alec to pray are met with failure. Instead of praying, Alec breaks into song, which distresses the priest who sees such behaviour as frivolous and inappropriate.

Alone in the days before his death, Alec looks back over his life and examines the series of events that have led him to this end.

KEY QUESTIONS

- From the very start of the novel, we know there is no hope for Alec. Does this affect your reading of the novel?

- What makes you want to read on?

- What do we learn about Alec's character from this brief opening?

- What are his views on life, family, religion, friendship and the army?

- How does the author convey so much in such a short introduction?

An Anglo-Irish stately home around 1911

Childhood in Wicklow

The young Alexander Moore is a lonely boy. He is the only child of Alicia and Frederick Moore, a wealthy Anglo-Irish couple who may have money but who have a loveless marriage.

Alec is not sent to school but is instead tutored at home by various ladies until the age of ten, and then by the local curate. His mother is determined to keep him at home instead of sending him to boarding school like other boys of his age. By refusing to allow Alec to leave, she deprives him of any chance of forming friendships with boys from a similar background to his own. Alec's father is a weak man, unable to stand up to his wife on this matter. It is clear that he is a pawn in some sort of game between his parents, and his happiness does not seem to concern his mother at all. She refuses to be left alone with her husband, whom she despises, so she keeps her son at home by claiming that he is delicate and in poor health. This is not true but Alec's father has given his word that the boy should be allowed to remain with his mother and she holds him to his word. Although Alec receives an adequate academic education from the curate, he misses out on the social aspect of school and admits that he lacks team spirit as a result.

Alec's mother is a very beautiful, cold, controlling, selfish woman. Alec's piano tutor is clearly captivated by her beauty, but nervous in her presence. She barely conceals her distaste for his shabby clothes and what she calls 'his appalling smell'. She insists that the tutor be dismissed, claiming she will teach Alec herself. She soon becomes impatient with her son's lack of talent, though, and that is an end to his piano lessons. Her selfishness is apparent in this early account of Alec's childhood; she does not take Alec's feelings into account at all and abandons her lessons with him when she becomes bored.

KEY QUESTIONS

- Alec is surrounded by adults. How do you think this affects his early childhood?

- Does he seem close to any of the adults in his life?

- Do you think he has any sort of relationship with his mother, his father or his tutor?

- Read the section of the book in which Alec tells of distressing Mr Bingham by pretending to struggle with his Latin translations. Does the young Alec seem like a typical young boy?

- If he had gone to school, do you think Alec would have learned more about life? If so, what sort of things might he have learned?

- If he had gone to school, do you think Alec would have been better at dealing with people later in life?

One of Alec's few pleasures is swimming in the lake near the house, a part of the Moores' estate. It is there, one day in May, that he meets Jerry Crowe. Jerry, who comes from a poor family in the village, spends most of his time in the Moores' stable yard, but he and Jerry have never spoken as it would not be deemed suitable for the son of the big house to be friendly with someone of Jerry's low social standing. When Jerry sees Alec watching him swimming in the lake, he calls out to the other boy, inviting him to join him in the water. Alec is indignant, accusing Jerry of trespassing. Jerry is undaunted by Alec's threat to have him prosecuted and repeats his invitation. Alec is not sure what to do at first, but eventually decides to join Jerry in the water. He finds that sharing the lake with another boy is far more fun than swimming alone. As the pair lie on the grass, drying off after their swim, they chat idly. Jerry is more confident and outgoing than Alec and seems unimpressed by the other boy's superior social position. He offers to teach Alec to fight if Alec will teach him how to ride a horse. Alec agrees and they shake on the bargain. This episode marks the beginning of the friendship between the two boys.

KEY QUESTIONS

- Why do you think Jerry is so much more confident than Alec?

- Is that what you would have expected, given their respective backgrounds?

- What is it about Jerry Crowe that attracts Alec to him?

- Alec has the benefit of a better academic education and a wealthier background than Jerry. What advantages, if any, does Jerry have over Alec?

Alec is delighted to have a friend at last, even though he knows that neither his family nor Jerry's would approve. The two boys keep their friendship a secret and meet by the lake or up on the hill behind the house. Alec keeps his word and teaches Jerry to ride and Jerry, for his part, teaches Alec to fight. When, in the days before his execution, Alec looks back on those summer days, he can only remember good times, although he knows that there must have been some occasions when he and Jerry did not get on. If there were, he cannot recall any of them now. His childhood friendship with Jerry was the only bright light in an otherwise dull and lonely life.

> Alec is delighted to have a friend at last, even though he knows that neither his family nor Jerry's would approve

As time moves on, the social gap between the two boys begins to become more apparent. As the book is a stream of memories, there are sudden jumps from Alec's early childhood to his teenage years. His memories focus on moments that were of great significance to him. Jerry has to leave school and get a job as a farm labourer to supplement his family's meagre income. His mother would like him to join the British army like his father as the money is good, but Jerry has no desire to be a soldier. Alec suggests that Jerry get a job in the Moores' stables, but Jerry claims that it would be difficult for them to be friends if he worked for Alec's family. Again, he reminds Alec of how much both of their families would disapprove of their friendship, and how his becoming an employee of Alec's family would only worsen the situation. The social divide between the pair is obvious and Jerry seems keenly aware of the fact.

Alec comes up with a plan for their future; he says that he will become a racehorse breeder and trainer and that Jerry can become his partner. Jerry is a little more realistic than Alec and doubts that such a thing could ever happen, but he agrees with his friend in order to keep him happy.

KEY QUESTIONS ❓

- **Why do you think Alec cannot remember any fights with Jerry?**
- **Do you think Jerry's other friends in the village would have been friendly with Alec? Why/why not?**
- **The happiness the boys share does not last and the real world intrudes on them. When does this happen?**
- **How does Alec react?**
- **Does he seem desperate to hold onto a dream of sorts?**
- **What is Alec's dream?**
- **Is it one Jerry shares?**

Jerry goes to work for one of the local farmers and the boys are not able to meet up as often as before. It seems to Alec that Jerry is growing up and becoming a man while he, Alec, is unchanged. Alec's life is static while Jerry's is moving on.

On the occasions when the boys do meet, they continue to discuss horse racing and they believe they are becoming quite expert on the topic. Alec still clings to the dream that he and Jerry will have a racing yard some day. In the meantime, Jerry manages to acquire a mare which he plans to ride in local races. It looks to be a tinker's pony and Alec suspects Jerry has stolen the horse. Jerry refuses to answer Alec's questions as to where he got the horse and is clearly delighted with his new mare. They christen her Queen Maeve and Jerry produces a

bottle of poteen so they can drink to her health. Alec asks him where he got the bottle of poteen and once again Jerry refuses to answer the question directly. Jerry seems to be becoming worldly wise and cunning, while Alec retains the relative innocence of childhood.

Alec seems quite content to plan his future with Jerry and to carry on meeting in secret to ride their horses in a makeshift arena in the hills, but Jerry is more aware of the outside world and how it might threaten their dream. He is keenly aware that Alec is heir to his father's estate and he asks Alec what he will do with it all when he comes into his inheritance. Alec hasn't thought

about that, instead concentrating on how he and Jerry will build their horse racing reputation. Jerry, more realistic than Alec, points out that their plans might be in danger as there is talk of an imminent war, but Alec dismisses the notion.

- Why do you think Alec has never thought about his inheritance?

 **KEY** QUESTIONS

- Do you think Alec is an unrealistic person? Why/why not?

The boys' friendship is discovered, though Alec never finds out exactly how his parents came to hear of it. Alec's mother calls him into the drawing room one day and asks him to accompany her on her daily walk to the lake to feed the swans. Alec is uncomfortable in her presence and he feels, as he always does, that she is not easy to converse with, being either distracted or appearing to want more from him than he can give. As they stroll, she brings up the subject of Jerry, referring to him dismissively as 'that person'. Alicia imperiously orders him to break any connection with the boy immediately. As they walk back towards the house, she observes that Alec is now a young man and that it is time he broadened his horizons. She announces her intention to take him with her on a tour of Europe. He is, she says, old enough to be a 'good companion' to her. Alec does not want to go but lacks the strength to stand up to his mother and resigns himself to travelling with her.

Later that evening, Alec's father calls him into the drawing room for a chat about his future. Both he and Alec find such conversations awkward and embarrassing. Frederick Moore realises that Alec is lonely and that his friendship with Jerry probably sprang from this loneliness. He casts around for ways to fill the void in his son's life, and suggests that perhaps he and Alec could get to know each other better.

Alec is pleased with his father's plans to allow him to help him with the hunt next season and to begin teaching him about the responsibilities of running the estate. He says he would like to begin helping his father immediately, but it is obvious that Alec's mother will not allow such a thing and has her mind set firmly on taking her son on a tour of Europe.

> Alec's mother is scornful of what she considers to be her husband's lack of authority when he is speaking to his son. She accuses him of being an 'ineffective man'

In desperation, Alec asks if it is wise to be travelling abroad when war is imminent. His mother scorns the very idea of war and astutely observes that this notion most likely came from Jerry. She repeats her demand that Alec have nothing more to do with 'that boy'. Alec's rather weak objections are overruled by his father, who sides with his mother, albeit with a slight reluctance.

Alec's mother is scornful of what she considers to be her husband's lack of authority when he is speaking to his son. She accuses him of being an 'ineffective man' and Alec's father does not argue. Alec feels sympathy for his aging, unhappy father, whose hand trembles as he picks up his pipe, and yet he cannot think of a good way to comfort the old man. He decides that the best way to ease the tension is to agree to his mother's plans.

The trip to Europe does not impress Alec and he uses only one short paragraph to describe it all. He and his mother return to Wicklow in the autumn and Alec is happy to be home again.

 **KEY QUESTIONS**

- **What do you think is Alicia's main reason for taking Alec to Europe?**

- **Do Alec's parents agree on anything?**

- **Alicia expects her husband and son to obey her, then seems to scorn them when they do. Do you think there is anything Alec or his father could do to please Alicia?**

Alec's father buys his son a beautiful chestnut mare. Alec is delighted with the horse but his mother is angry that the mare excites Alec far more than his trip to Europe.

It is not until the following spring that Alec gets a chance to speak to Jerry again. Jerry wins the local point-to-point and Alec's father presents him with the prize. Alec also shakes his hand and congratulates him, but there is a distance between them now. Jerry calls Alec 'sir' and seems unwilling to chat with his old friend. However, Alec's enthusiastic praise of Jerry's horse breaks the ice and Jerry, in turn, compliments Alec's new mare. Before they can really catch up, Alec's mother takes him away. She is furious that Alec still seems fond of Jerry and tells her son that Jerry is a most unsuitable friend. She claims that Jerry is involved with 'some criminal organisation' bent on overthrowing British rule in Ireland.

As the months pass, Alec and his father grow closer, while his mother watches with anger and bitterness. Alec senses that beneath his mother's superficial beauty and charm lies a deep 'black burning rage which constantly consumed her'.

War breaks out but it initially has little impact on the lives of the Moore family. Alec's father thinks those who encourage young Irish men to join up are 'bloody fools' but Alec's mother admires them. This difference of opinion seems to worry Alec's father as he does not want his own son to join

Alec's father thinks those who encourage young Irish men to join up are 'bloody fools' but Alec's mother admires them

the army. This worry takes its toll; the old man ages visibly and his health begins to fail as the war continues. Matters come to a head when a local man is killed and Alec's mother is clearly excited by the attention his death generates. She announces that Alec will soon be going to war. Frederick is unable to stand up to his wife, even though he is horrified at the thought of Alec leaving to join the army.

KEY QUESTIONS

- Why does Alicia want Alec to join the army?

- What reasons can you think of for her determination to send her son to the front?

When Alec's mother leaves the room, his father begins to talk about his failed marriage and the hatred his wife feels for him. He says that this hatred is the real reason she wants Alec to join the army. She knows that depriving him of his son and sending the boy into a situation in which he may be killed will hurt her husband deeply. Alec says that he will not go, but his father says that he will, as Alec is a coward. He doesn't say this cruelly, but in a matter of fact way. Alec points out that a coward would stay at home, but his father says that cowards are more afraid to face life than death. Alec is puzzled by this comment and repeats his assertion that he is not going anywhere. His father says nothing more about the war, but seems resigned to the fact of his son's joining up. He talks some more about his failed marriage and Alec leaves him sitting by the fire, drinking himself into a stupor.

KEY QUESTIONS

- What do you think Frederick means when he says that cowards are more afraid to face life than death?

- Do you agree with him? Explain why/why not.

- How does Frederick Moore react to what he sees as the inevitability of his son's departure?

- Is this in keeping with his behaviour so far?

- Do you think either parent puts Alec's feelings before their own?

When Alec reaches his bedroom, he finds his mother waiting for him. She asks him again to join the army, saying that it means a lot to her. When he refuses, she calls him a coward. Alec does not rise to this bait and repeats his refusal. He points out that his father needs him. His mother seems angered by his fondness for his father and tells her son that she sacrificed any chances of happiness by staying with her husband for his sake. All she asks for in return, she says, is that he should join the army. Again, Alec refuses to go.

Now Alec's mother plays her trump card. Cruelly, she tells Alec that Frederick Moore is not his father, although the old man does not know it. Alec is horrified and asks who his real father is. His mother says that he is dead and that she barely remembers him anyway. She admits that she is 'not a nice woman' but claims that it is partly her unhappy life that has made her this way. She leaves, saying as she does so that her wish for Alec to join the army is motivated by 'all the right reasons as well as a few of the wrong ones'.

KEY QUESTIONS

- Do you believe Alicia when she says that Frederick Moore is not Alec's father?

- Why did she choose this moment to tell Alec this fact?

- Do you think that Alicia is telling the truth when she says that some of the reasons she wants Alec to join the army are 'the right reasons'?

Alec is deeply upset by the news that the man who raised him is not his real father. He leaves the house and walks down the path towards the village. He is lonely and distressed and in need of 'God or a friend'. When he draws near to the village, Alec finds that a group of local people are drinking and dancing at the crossroads. Jerry Crowe is in the group of villagers and he approaches Alec. The pair drink and chat and Jerry tells Alec that he is enlisting in the army the following day. He says that he needs the cash but hints that there is also another reason. Alec is surprised that his old friend is joining the British army and says that he thought Jerry was 'with the Shinners'. By this, Alec means Sinn Féin. Jerry reacts violently to this comment about the republican movement and tells Alec to shut up. Alec is taken aback and Jerry quickly recovers himself, saying that he is a little drunk and insisting that it is only cash that is making him join the army. Alec tells Jerry that he too is planning to enlist the following day.

Alec tells Jerry about his mother's claim that he is not his father's son. Jerry suspects that Mrs Moore may be lying and he says that women say what they want to get what they want.

Alec becomes quite drunk and Jerry decides to help him home. They half walk, half crawl along the path towards the lake. In an effort to sober up a little, they go for a swim. It is almost morning when they get out of the lake and dry themselves.

The pair chat for a while longer about girls and the likelihood of the war being over by Christmas until Alec complains of the cold and says it's time to go. Jerry says that they will meet tomorrow at the train but that Alec will probably be travelling first class. Alec disagrees, but Jerry is more realistic about the differences between an officer and an ordinary enlisted man.

KEY QUESTIONS

- How would you describe Jerry's attitude towards women?
- Why do you think Jerry gets so angry when Alec asks him if he is 'with the Shinners'?

Alec gets up late the next morning. He is hungover and still slightly drunk. He dresses with care as he knows his mother will not tolerate anything but an 'immaculate appearance' at the breakfast table. This is typical of the Moore family; appearance is all. On the surface, they are perfect. Alec reflects that his parents will probably 'grow old immaculately, their implacable hatred of each other hidden from the world'. When he appears at breakfast, his mother seems pleased to see him and acts as if nothing has changed between them after their conversation of the previous night. She holds her face up for a kiss but Alec is disgusted at the thought of touching her and ignores her gesture. His father seems to have retreated into himself once again. He is reading the paper and merely grunts when Alec enters the room.

Alec feels unwell after his excesses of the previous night and decides against eating breakfast. His mother observes this with displeasure and accuses him of refusing to eat because he is 'sulking'. She changes the subject by announcing that Alec's cousin Maud is coming to stay. Alec says she can take his horse if she wants to hunt as he is joining the army immediately. His parents are surprised as they did not think he would be leaving so soon. However, their reactions differ in that his father is clearly distressed at the thought of his son leaving, while his mother views his decision to leave so quickly as further proof that he is sulking. Still, for all her seeming annoyance, Alec senses that she is triumphant. He is going. She has won.

Alicia says that she is proud of her son but Alec laughs derisively. He knows that she views this as a personal victory and that she is unconcerned for him, whatever she might say.

At his father's request, Alec goes to the study to talk to him before he leaves. His father gives him some money, apologising that it is not more. He tells Alec that he will give him more money whenever he needs it. Frederick also gives his son his pocket watch. It is a family heirloom and a sign of his father's love, whatever he might say about 'sentimental gestures' not suiting either of them. The watch is warm from the heat of his father's body and Alec puts it in his pocket. In a way, the warm, ticking watch is a symbol of Alec's father's heart, and it is all he can give his son in these final moments of their parting.

> Alicia says that she is proud of her son but Alec laughs derisively

In the drawing room, Alec's mother says goodbye to her son in a theatrical, showy way. Her expressions of love seem shallow and selfish compared to Alec's father's unemotional but clearly heartfelt goodbye.

- Why do you think Alec decided to join the army so quickly?
- Is there any positive female role model for Alec?
- Do you think this is likely to affect him emotionally?
- Do you think his mother will be happy now that Alec has finally agreed to join up?

 **KEY QUESTIONS**

British army recruitment poster, 1916

The six weeks of basic training on the shores of Belfast Lough pass without incident. As usual, Alec seems oddly detached from it all, regarding it as a sort of 'mad children's game, except that the rules had to be taken seriously'. Jerry's prophecy that Alec would be made an officer proves correct. That December, 1914, Alec's commanding officer Major Glendinning sends for him and tells him that they are all, Major Glendinning included, to leave for the front the next day. Alec notes the major's self-control, and also his contempt for the Irish enlisted men in his charge. Rather surprisingly, the seemingly tough and unfeeling Major Glendinning offers Alec some time off the following day to visit his family. Alec refuses and the major seems indifferent to his decision. However, as Alec goes to leave, Major Glendinning calls him back again and tells him that he has noticed Alec's aloofness and his unwillingness to mix with his fellow officers. He is clearly displeased that the war has caused men like Alec, 'the wrong type', to train as soldiers. As Alec leaves the major's office, the enlisted man on duty outside grins and winks at him. Alec has neither the respect of his commanding officer nor the enlisted men.

> Glendinning is clearly displeased that the war has caused men like Alec, 'the wrong type', to train as soldiers

Alec meets Jerry briefly before they set sail for Belgium but Jerry is keenly aware that an officer should not be seen to be chatting to an enlisted man. They part ways and the Irish contingent sets sail from Dublin the next day.

- What is Alec's attitude towards army life?
- Is there any indication of the type of soldier he is likely to become?
- What is your initial impression of Major Glendinning?

KEY
QUESTIONS

The men reach Belgium and set up their base in a derelict farmhouse in West Outre. The weather is dismal and the rain and filth make conditions miserable.

Alec is joined by another young officer called Bennett. They are roughly the same age, although Bennett, like Jerry, seems more worldly-wise than Alec.

On the third morning after their arrival at the farmhouse, the sun comes out, and Bennett suggests they go horse riding. Alec is dubious, thinking that Major Glendinning might not approve, but Bennett points out that he need never know. Cheered, Alec asks if a friend can join them. Bennett agrees and Alec goes to fetch Jerry.

Alec introduces Jerry to Bennett and Bennett shakes Jerry's hand graciously, seemingly indifferent to the fact that Alec's friend is an enlisted man. Alec warms to Bennett for this simple act of decency. The three men ride to the top of a hill and look down on the scene Bennett has brought them to see; what he calls his 'show'. It is the front line of the battle raging at Ypres. Bennett is impressed by it all and says that his life to date has been predictable and dull, and that the war is the best thing that has ever happened to him. He doesn't seem to care whether he becomes a hero or dies; either is preferable to leading a tedious life.

As the men ride back towards the farmhouse, they are confronted by a 'small irate major' who says he will report them to their commanding officer, Major Glendinning, for taking the horses and riding out for pleasure. He is particularly annoyed to see that Bennett and Alec have brought an enlisted man along with them. His accusation, 'I suppose you think you're here for fun', shocks Bennett and the whole incident brings an unpleasant note of reality into what had been a lighthearted and enjoyable excursion.

KEY QUESTIONS

- What is your initial impression of Bennett?

- What is Bennett's attitude towards the war?

- Do you think Bennett is likely to make a good soldier? Why/why not?

The next day the men go to the front line. The system is that they spend three days in the trenches at the front, then withdraw to the support trenches for three days before returning to the front line again. Every two weeks or so the men go back to the farmhouse for five or six days' rest. Life in the trenches is horrific. The trenches are filled with mud, sewage and the remains of dead soldiers. Alec admits that he is constantly frightened but says what frightens him most is not the thought of death, but the thought that he might come to accept this way of life as normal. He and Bennett share a dug-out which, though it does have dry straw on the floor, is also a home to rats. Bennett seems oblivious to the discomfort and sleeps soundly. Alec is not so lucky. He is plagued by nightmares and by the physical discomfort of chilblains rubbed raw by his boots. In a way, he welcomes the pain as it distracts him from the horror around him.

Bennett's view of the war is a cynical one. He tells Alec that whether they live or die is up to the whims of the 'fat men at home' and their German counterparts. The soldiers, he claims, are like performing dogs, trained to do whatever their masters want. He also observes that, while the men like Alec, they wouldn't follow him into battle. Neither would they follow Bennett himself, whom the men dislike. But, he reasons, they would do whatever Major Glendinning said because 'the dogs trust the whip crackers'.

KEY QUESTIONS

- Do you agree with Bennett's rather cynical view of the world?
- Do you agree with him about Major Glendinning's power over the men?
- How is Alec coping with life in the trenches?
- Why do you think Bennett is less affected by the discomfort and the horror than Alec is?

Alec leaves Bennett sleeping in the dug-out and he goes out into the trenches to find Jerry. His friend is standing in a foot and a half of water at the furthest end of one of the trenches. Alec gives him some rum to warm him up and they chat for a while. Their conversation is ended by the appearance of Major Glendinning, who has had his attention drawn to Alec's absence by Sergeant Barry. The sergeant has told the major that Alec has been at the far end of the trench for some time and he says that he fears he may be in trouble. The more likely reason for his alerting the major is to get Alec into trouble for fraternising with an enlisted man. The major exchanges a brief word with Jerry, then calls Alec to follow him into his dug-out.

Major Glendinning reprimands Alec for talking to Jerry, and tells him very forcefully that he will not tolerate such behaviour. He says that he insists on 'impersonal discipline' at all times. The major is clearly disgusted to be in charge of a group of amateur soldiers, particularly as they are 'damn bog Irish'. He intends, nonetheless, to turn them all into professional soldiers and he tells Alec to pass the same message on to Bennett.

KEY QUESTIONS

- Why is Major Glendinning not in favour of officers fraternising with enlisted men?

- Do you agree with him that 'impersonal discipline' is the best way to lead the men?

- Do you think Alec is likely to obey the major?

Five days later, the men are back at the West Outre farmhouse for a break from the trenches. Bennett tells Alec that he has arranged another horse riding trip. Alec is reluctant, reminding Bennett that Major Glendinning expressly forbade such an outing. Bennett does not care and he tells Alec that Jerry is all set to join them. Alec admits that he finds it 'hard to break the rules' but Bennett is contemptuous of rules, telling Alec that by not going to school, he missed out on the chance to develop a 'healthy disrespect for authority'.

Bennett is fond of Alec and he seems to want more than just casual friendship. He tells Alec that he had 'never expected to admire gentleness in a man', and puts his hand on Alec's head in a gesture that is a 'cross between a benediction and a caress'. Alec is unsure how to react, even though he knows that some sort of reaction would be appropriate. He is confused by Bennett's affection because it is not something he is used to. Coming from a loveless home, he regards warmth and spontaneity as dangerous qualities. The moment passes and Bennett changes the subject.

- What is Alec's attitude towards rules and regulations?

- He says he finds it difficult to break them, but do you think he has any respect for the rules?

- Do you think that Bennett is right and that going to school would have helped Alec to cope more easily with army life?

- What sort of relationship do you think Bennett wants with Alec?

KEY QUESTIONS

Alec, Bennett and Jerry head off on horseback as before. The three men ride on until they reach a village. Jerry suggests stopping for a drink in a bar and the other two agree.

As they sit in the bar, Bennett asks Jerry if he is a Home Ruler. Jerry scorns the idea of Home Rule and tells Bennett that he is a republican. Bennett is interested but wonders why Jerry is fighting for the British in this war if he regards them as the enemy. Jerry explains that he regards his time in the British army as training for when he returns home. He thinks that, with his experience, he will be very useful to the republican army when the time comes. He seems determined to follow Padraig Pearse and to fight for Ireland's freedom. Alec has never heard Jerry talk this way before and refuses to believe that these extreme republican views are shared by many others. He says that, for his part, his only dream is to have a racing yard with Jerry. The three men are becoming a little drunk and it is obviously time to go.

- Why do you think Jerry tells Bennett his plans to fight for the republican cause?

- How does Alec respond to this admission?

KEY QUESTIONS

The following morning Major Glendinning addresses the men before they go back to the front. He tells them that when the time comes to fight, he will expect them all to do their duty and he will have 'no scruples about meting out the ultimate' to any man who does not do what is expected of him. Alec believes him and hopes that the men do, too. As a matter of form, Major Glendinning asks if anyone has any questions. Jerry steps forward and says that he would like to transfer to the horse lines. The major is not impressed, wondering how Jerry managed to go and see the horse lines without permission and also accusing him of looking for an easier role in the war. Jerry protests, explaining that the horses are in a bad way and that he could help. Major Glendinning refuses him permission to transfer and says that he has had his eye on Jerry for some time as a 'potential trouble-maker'. He tells Sergeant Barry, who does not like Jerry, to keep an eye on him, too.

At breakfast in the farmhouse, Alec reads a letter from his mother. She talks about wounded soldiers coming home to Wicklow and speaks of the war as if it were a rather jolly adventure. Alec's lack of letter-writing offends his mother, who wants to have a connection to the war and to be able to share her news with others. There is no mention of genuine concern for Alec or of wanting to be reassured that he is well. Ironically, for someone safe at home in Ireland, she tells her son that she is 'quite wounded' by his silence.

Bennett tries to talk to Alec, but Alec tells him to be quiet as he is reading a letter from home. Without warning, Bennett takes Alec's letter and tears it into tiny pieces, throwing the scraps on the floor behind him. Alec does not react and Bennett asks him why he doesn't. Alec has no answer to this question. It seems as though Bennett wants to provoke Alec into some kind of reaction, some kind of show of emotion or passion, but he is unable to rouse the other man out of his habitually quiet, gentle state. He leaves and Alec turns to the task of writing back to his mother. He focuses his attention on the wooden farmhouse table and decides to write 'a detailed description' of it to his mother. It is as if by concentrating on something so unemotional and meaningless, he can block out all the disturbing thoughts that might otherwise trouble him.

KEY QUESTIONS

• **Do you think that Major Glendinning was right and that Jerry was looking for an easy job?**

• **Do you think Alec should have spoken up on Jerry's behalf?**

- Is there a sense of rising tension as the major's dislike for Jerry increases?

- What does the major say he will do to anyone who disobeys the order to fight? Do you believe him?

- Why does Bennett tear up Alec's letter?

- Does he manage to provoke the response he wanted?

- What do you think of Alec's reply to his mother's letter?

Troops marching back to the front lines

The men march back to the front lines. Alec again finds conditions appalling. The trenches are in even worse repair than usual and have obviously sustained some heavy shelling. Somewhere in No Man's Land, a man is screaming in agony. The men in the trenches are tormented by the sound, as is Alec.

Just as Alec is about to settle down for the night, Jerry appears in his dug-out, carrying a cup of tea. Alec apologises for not speaking up for him when he asked to transfer to the horse lines but Jerry tells him not to worry about it, that it wouldn't have made any difference. Alec produces a flask of rum and the two men share it. As they drink, Jerry tells Alec that he tried to shoot the screaming, dying man, but couldn't get him in his rifle sights as it was too dark.

In an effort to distract themselves, Alec and Jerry try to remember pleasant things about home: grass, silence, swans and turf fires. The talk turns to their fellow soldiers. Jerry clearly hates Major Glendinning and remarks that when he is fighting for the republican cause, he will 'have a bullet or two for the likes of him'. Alec wonders how Jerry can contemplate fighting again after all they have seen at the front. Jerry says that the two things are totally different and that his fight will be a guerilla war, with no trenches and no front lines. He is excited at the thought but Alec can't share his delight. Jerry assures him that he will come around to his way of thinking in the fullness of time and says that they will need each other when the fight for freedom begins. Alec is unhappy at the thought of another war and says so to Jerry. He accuses Jerry of liking violence and when Jerry points out that Alec likes hunting, which is a violent activity, Alec has to admit he hadn't thought of that. He wonders if his inability to 'think things out very clearly' stems from a 'kind of lack of energy'.

Bennett arrives the next morning. He is cheerful and brisk initially but his good humour vanishes at the sound of the injured man's screams.

KEY QUESTIONS

- Alec says that he suffers from 'a kind of lack of energy' which prevents him from seeing things clearly. Does this remind you of his father, who said that when he 'can have no possible influence a terrible lethargy sets in'?

- Is Alec a man of action, do you think? Is Jerry? Is Bennett?

At dark, Major Glendinning arrives. He exchanges a few words with Alec and then notices the piles of paper on which Alec has been writing. He shows an interest but Alec plays down his efforts and stuffs the paper into his kit-bag.

Alec goes to find some bedding for the major, who has decided to stay the night. At that moment, the wounded soldier in No Man's Land begins screaming again and Major Glendinning, hearing it, calls Alec to explain. Alec tells him that the man is from the Gloucestershire Regiment and that he has been lying there for four days now. Alec says that he doubts the man is conscious. Major Glendinning says that he and Alec will go and 'see to' the man when the major has finished his report. Alec is taken aback, and wonders aloud what they can do for the man. Major Glendinning says that they won't know until they get there and find out all the facts. He dismisses Alec and gets on with his report.

Alec tries to read a book while the major writes but he is unable to concentrate. He is terrified at the thought of seeing the man's injuries and terrified that he will end up the same way.

The major finishes his report and in a brisk, matter-of-fact manner, makes preparations for what he calls the 'outing'. He shows no sign of any emotion, merely saying to the men that if he and Alec should not return, Mr Bennett should be summoned to replace them. The major says that they will either bring the wounded man back or ... He leaves the sentence unfinished, but it is obvious he means that he will end the man's suffering if he has to. Alec and Major Glendinning head out into No Man's Land. They reach the injured soldier and the major looks at the extent of his injuries, swears, and removes papers from the soldier's pocket, giving them to Alec for safekeeping. He draws his knife, quietly. Alec quotes a line of Yeats' poetry but the major tells him to shut up. There is a sigh from the major at the moment the man's screaming stops. While Alec does not describe what has happened, it is obvious the major has ended the man's life. (He could not have shot him, as the sound of a handgun in No Man's Land would have drawn enemy gunfire.)

He draws his knife, quietly. Alec quotes a line of Yeats' poetry but the major tells him to shut up

Alec and the major return quickly to their trench. He and Alec go to the dug-out and Alec changes out of his wet clothes, wrapping himself in his coat. The major sits at his table and begins to clean his bloody knife with a spotless white handkerchief. Alec sees that such a practical, emotionless task is necessary to the major, perhaps to help him to focus on something other than the killing of the wounded man. The major turns his attention to Alec again and accuses him of being a dismal creature. He is disgusted that Alec began reciting poetry when they were dealing with the injured soldier. He sees this as weakness.

He says that prayers and poetry are the same thing and that he has 'no time for the man who cannot face reality'. Alec's protestation that all men may have a different view of reality is rubbished by the major, who goes on to say that he has heard Alec never went to school. He feels that this was a 'grave error' and tells Alec that boarding school teaches boys how to 'accept the burdens of manhood'.

KEY QUESTIONS

- What do you think of Major Glendinning's decision to finish writing his report before going out to deal with the wounded soldier?

- Do you think he did the right thing for the injured man?

- Why did he do what he did?

- Do you think it affected him at all?

- What was Alec's reaction?

- Major Glendinning, like Bennett, thinks Alec should have been sent to school. Do you agree with them?

The next three days at the front line are spent extending the trench by fifteen yards. On the fourth day, Jerry visits Alec in the dug-out and they share a drink. Both men are ill and exhausted from their time at the front line but Alec seems to be taking it worse. Jerry realises this and, without being asked, takes Alec's boots off and rubs some alcohol into his aching, swollen feet.

Four days later Alec and his men leave the front and go back to the farm for a rest. They hear that the Allied forces have suffered huge losses along the line from them, but they are almost numb to such news now as they are constantly in the presence of death. Christmas comes and goes with no sense of celebration.

Alec receives a letter from his father saying that Alec's last letter home to his mother, in which he described the table in great detail, upset her greatly. Alec's father found it amusing but nonetheless asks if Alec will write her a proper letter. The letter is short and unemotional, although there is a sense, as there always is with Alec's father, that he would like to be able to say more. The letter unsettles Alec a little and he tells Bennett that he would like to 'remain untouched' by everything around him. Bennett is puzzled by this remark and claims not to understand Alec at all.

The six days at the farm are spent drilling and repairing uniforms and equipment under the eagle eye of Major Glendinning. On the last night before they leave for the front again, Alec and Bennett return to their room to find Jerry waiting for them. He is agitated and wants to speak to Alec in private. Bennett assures them that he is not listening and Jerry tells Alec that he needs some time off. Jerry's mother has written to him saying that his father is missing in action. She asks Jerry to go and find out what has happened to him.

Alec says he will write to his father to ask him to help Jerry's family if they are in financial difficulties now that Jerry's father is no longer sending money home, but Jerry doesn't seem to want that. He wants to search for his father and asks Alec to speak to the major on his behalf. Alec doesn't think this will do much good but he says he will try. He leaves Jerry in his room with the sleeping Bennett and goes to see Major Glendinning.

Major Glendinning does not seem to care about Jerry's situation and says that Jerry may not have leave to go and look for his father. He also tells Alec that it is time he ended his friendship with Jerry. The major points out, quite reasonably, that Jerry is not the only one with missing family members and that to accommodate his request would set a dangerous precedent. This is another example of the major's seemingly uncaring decisions being based on the necessity of keeping the army running as smoothly as possible.

When Alec tells Jerry the news, it seems that Jerry had predicted the major's response. Alec is worried that Jerry will take matters into his own hands and go absent without leave. He is relieved to see Jerry with the rest of the men the following morning. The day is cold and wet but when Alec asks the major if the men can have a break and a cup of tea before the six- or seven-hour march, the major refuses. Alec senses that this is because he, Alec, is ineffectual. He says that if Bennett or Sergeant Barry had made the same request, it would have been granted.

KEY QUESTIONS

- **Do you think Alec is a good friend to Jerry?**
- **Do you agree with Major Glendinning's decision not to allow Jerry to search for his father?**
- **Do you agree that Alec is ineffectual?**

The days at the front are dreadful. Up until this time, Alec and his men have avoided heavy fire but now they are attacked relentlessly. It is not until they return to the farmhouse that Alec notices Jerry's absence. He asks Bennett if he has seen him but Bennett doesn't take much notice as he is ill. He has a fever and is taken to the base hospital the following day.

Sergeant Barry comes to Alec later that morning to report Jerry's absence. He seems to think that Alec might know something about it and he seems to take a malicious pleasure in reminding Alec that Jerry will be executed when he is caught.

Major Glendinning sends for Alec and he too asks Alec what he knows about Jerry's running away. Alec is defensive and the major reminds him that Jerry has a bad record already. He is suspicious of Jerry's political leanings and tells Alec that he knows 'as well as the next man what goes on in your treacherous little country'. He thinks that many of the Irish are traitors who may well side with the Germans and he asks if Alec thinks Jerry has joined the enemy. Alec says he presumes Jerry has gone to search for his father. Major Glendinning, true to Sergeant Barry's word, says that if Jerry is found, he will be charged with 'desertion in the face of enemy fire'.

Alec struggles to understand what Jerry thinks he will achieve by deserting. He feels sorry for the other man, imagining him turning over corpses in a futile search for his father. Alec thinks of the times he and Jerry shared together in the Wicklow hills and he reflects on the fact that he never wanted to find out what lay beyond the hills. He was content in his sheltered world, and now that he has seen the horrors of the world outside his homeland, he is sorrier than ever that he left.

KEY QUESTIONS

- How do you think Bennett's absence will affect Alec?
- Do you think Bennett would have helped or spoken up for Jerry? Why/why not?
- Can you see any parallels between Alicia Moore and Major Glendinning?

That night Alec is woken from his sleep by Jerry. Jerry has returned, soaking wet and chilled to the bone. Alec gives him some of Bennett's dry clothes and tells him to get into his warm bed. He offers Jerry some brandy, and they lie together in the bed for warmth as Jerry tells him what he has been up to. Jerry seems concerned that his absence may have caused trouble for Alec but Alec is not worried about that. He is bewildered by Jerry's decision to return, knowing that a court martial and a possible death sentence awaits.

As Jerry and Alec lie together, Jerry tells Alec that he did find out about his father. Mr Crowe stepped on a landmine and was killed. Jerry is not unduly upset, explaining that he never knew his father well as the man only came home from the army occasionally.

Alec is concerned for Jerry and tries to formulate a plan of escape. Jerry seems content to face whatever punishment is coming. He has done what his mother asked and he is pleased that he did what he needed to do. The pair chat about the future, even though they are both keenly aware that they may have no future. Jerry plans to settle down with a comfortable widow. Alec plans to live alone.

There is movement downstairs and both men know that Jerry will soon be found. For once, Jerry has nothing to suggest and admits to Alec that he is frightened. This is a reversal of the way things usually are between Alec and Jerry. Exhausted, emotionally drained and despairing, Jerry asks Alec to help him. Alec cannot think of any solution to the mess in which they find themselves, so he decides that Jerry should face up to whatever is coming.

Alec gets up and gets dressed while Jerry lies in the bed, drinking brandy. Fear makes Jerry drink himself into insensibility. Moments after he falls asleep, a soldier O'Keefe enters the room. He sees Jerry in the bed and seems sympathetic to the situation. He advises Alec to go for a walk so that Jerry can be smuggled out of the bedroom. The soldier realises that if Jerry is found in Alec's room, Alec will be guilty of harbouring a deserter. Their plan is foiled when Sergeant Barry opens the door just as Alec is about to leave. The soldiers accompanying him drag Jerry from the room and Barry leaves, clearly contemptuous of both Alec and Jerry. O'Keefe sees that Alec is deeply shocked by Jerry's arrest, and he wraps a blanket around him and promises a fire and a cup of tea.

KEY QUESTIONS

- **What do you think of Alec's reaction to Jerry's return?**
- **Do you think he has really faced the fact that Major Glendinning will have Jerry shot for desertion?**
- **Why did Jerry return if he knew he would be arrested?**

Alec is summoned by Major Glendinning. The major gets straight to the point and says that it is very odd that Jerry was found in Alec's room. Jerry's arrest seems to have had a powerful affect on Alec. In the past he was reasonably polite to Major Glendinning but now he seems not to care about anything at all. When the major reminds him that they are fighting a war and asks him if he realises what he is wearing, Alec replies: 'Some sort of fancy dress, sir.' This lack of respect for uniform and country pushes the major beyond the limit of his endurance. He strikes Alec across the face with his cane and seems to be struggling to maintain any sort of self-control.

The major tries once more to speak to Alec about his attitude. He says that he dislikes 'public confrontation with one of my officers'. He is concerned that such disagreements cause problems for the men's morale. Alec is alarmed to hear that Major Glendinning will be compiling a report on Jerry's desertion, as he knows the major dislikes Jerry. He tries to say a few words in Jerry's defence, but the major will hear none of it. He tells Alec that there is an attack planned soon and that there can be no 'flaw in the machinery'. Alec protests that the soldiers are men, not machines, but the major disagrees. He regards Alec's arguments against war as childish and pointless.

While he comes across as forceful and unemotional, there are hints that the major occasionally struggles to keep his tough, calm exterior. As Alec leaves, he sees the major covering his eyes with his right hand, a gesture of despair or tiredness, and Alec is touched. He cannot work out whether he hates or respects the major and he wonders if he will ever be able to see things clearly.

- Why do you think the major reacts so strongly to Alec's remark about the army uniform?

- Alec cannot decide if he hates or respects Major Glendinning. What is your opinion of the major so far?

- Do you think Alec will ever achieve his aim of seeing things clearly?

? KEY QUESTIONS

The following day, as Alec is marching with his weary, demoralised and footsore men, two low-flying swans pass by. Alec stops to watch them and feels a little 'embarrassed by their presence', as if they were old friends who had visited at an inconvenient moment. However, as he raises a hand to greet them, one of his men fires his pistol at the birds and the leading swan crashes to the ground, dead. Alec is appalled but the men can't understand why he should care. This is understandable, as they have been forced to face far worse horrors than this during their time at the front. Life is cheap to these men now.

KEY QUESTIONS ❓
- What do the swans represent?
- Why do you think Alec reacts so strongly to the death of the swan?

Sergeant Barry is waiting for them when they get back to the farm. He tells Alec that the major wants a word with him. Major Glendinning says that Jerry has been sentenced to death and that Alec is to command the firing squad the following morning. Alec can barely take in the news. Major Glendinning tells him that Jerry's execution is necessary if there is to be 'no crumbling of the men's morale'. This seems an odd thing to say, as having one of their number executed would surely damage the soldiers' spirits. However, the only aspect of the men's morale the major is interested in is their willingness to obey orders. Alec rejects the major's logic and refuses to accept that Jerry is a deserter or a possible traitor. The major says that Alec refuses to 'be guided' and Alec retorts that the major refuses 'to view people as anything but cattle'. The major seems unmoved by this accusation and says that Alec may come around to his way of thinking some day.

The thought of ordering his men to shoot Jerry horrifies Alec and he tells the major that he won't do it. The major says that, in that case, he will have Alec executed, too. Alec asks the major how he became so evil and the major, seeming not to take offence at the question, replies that the world taught him and that it will also teach Alec in time. Alec finally seems to accept that there is no hope for Jerry. Major Glendinning is pleased. The major seems to think that he has succeeded in convincing Alec of the necessity of Jerry's execution and, in what he clearly imagines is kindly advice, he advises Alec to make sure that his men shoot straight so that Jerry is killed as quickly and cleanly as possible.

- Do you think Major Glendinning is evil?
- Why do you think the major tries to talk Alec around to his way of thinking?
- What is the major's view of sentiment?
- Do you agree with his view?

KEY QUESTIONS

Alec goes straight to the detention camp to visit Jerry. Jerry says that the waiting is torturous and that he can't think of anything to think about. They reminisce about the past: the lake, the swans, their plans to start a racing yard together. Alec takes out his revolver and asks Jerry to play a tune on his mouth organ. Jerry says that he can't, as they took everything away from him in case he committed suicide and 'spoiled their fun'. Alec asks him to sing a song instead and Jerry breaks into a verse of 'The Croppy Boy', an old song about a young Irish rebel who was executed by the British.

While Jerry sings, Alec reaches out with his left hand and takes Jerry's hand in his. Jerry looks straight into Alec's eyes and smiles. As

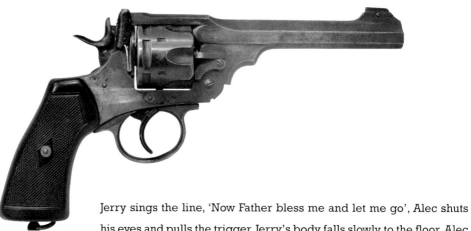

Jerry sings the line, 'Now Father bless me and let me go', Alec shuts his eyes and pulls the trigger. Jerry's body falls slowly to the floor. Alec hears the sound of soldiers running towards the room.

 **KEY QUESTIONS**

- Do you think Alec did the right thing? Why/why not?
- Was it a brave act?
- Were you surprised that he did it?
- Do you think Jerry's choice of song was appropriate?

The book ends where it began. Alec is sitting in the detention camp, awaiting his own execution. As he is 'an officer and a gentleman' they have left him his pen. So he sits and waits and writes.

KEY QUESTIONS

- What do you think of the structure of the book?
- Did the fact that you knew Alec's fate at the start of the book add to or take from your enjoyment of the story?
- Did you like the ending?
- Could you think of any other ending which would not have compromised the integrity of the principal characters?

The trenches were little more than drains, thick with mud, rubbish and sewage

Character
analysis

2

Alec Moore

First impression

Alec Moore narrates this story from his prison cell. He is alone and awaiting execution. He claims that he is 'committed to no cause', loves 'no living person' and has 'no future except what you can count in hours'. He is unwilling to contact his parents to tell them about his impending death, preferring to leave it to the War Office. The picture we are presented with at the start of the book is of a man who has nothing to live for, a man who is completely alone.

Does not have a normal childhood

Life in the Moore household is filled with polite hostility and deep bitterness. Alec's parents are so caught up in their own problems that they barely seem to notice their son at times. And when they do, he is not much better off. Young Alec's function is to be a shield between his parents and a sort of hostage who can be used by his mother to further her own plans.

Because Alicia is determined to keep Alec with her and not to allow him to attend school, Alec's life remains almost unbearably dull. While Jerry moves on and grows up, nothing seems to change for Alec. This cloistered existence means that Alec is quite naïve in some ways, compared to his more experienced friend.

Although he has had plenty of experience of the unhappiness of the adult world, Alec rather childishly believes that if he follows his dream, he will have a happy future running a horse racing yard with Jerry. Jerry goes along with the dream, but is more cynical and worldly-wise and says several times that Alec is 'a great one for thinking things will be easy'.

Detached observer rather than participant

Alec's unhappy, cold, lonely, loveless upbringing turns him into someone who has 'developed the technique of listening to a fine art'. He claims that he 'could become at will as still and invisible as a chair or a bowl of flowers'. His parents often seem unaware of his presence, so absorbed are they in their own affairs. They forget that Alec is there when they begin to argue with one another. As a result, the silent youngster hears more than he should and is keenly aware of his parents' dysfunctional relationship.

Living in a household that is filled with silence and bitterness, young Alec retreats into himself and watches the world somewhat dispassionately. He does not view adults as people with whom he can interact meaningfully but instead observes them in a rather detached way.

So emotionally scarred that he fears being close to anyone

Jerry may show Alec the happiness of friendship but he also shows him the heartbreak, which is something Alec has always feared. At the start of his friendship with Jerry he says that their time together 'snatched me from the passive solicitude of my normal life, warned me of the pleasure and the fear of living'. Later on, when he and Jerry are discussing their theoretical future together in the moments before Jerry is arrested for desertion, Alec says that he wants to live alone and that he is 'only afraid' when he is 'with other people'. This attitude is hardly surprising, given that Alec's father has outlined for his son the loneliness and the misery of living with a scornful and contemptuous spouse.

> Alec says that he wants to live alone and that he is 'only afraid' when he is 'with other people'

Frederick also astutely notes that Alec fears life. This, he claims, is why Alec will go to war. Death is easier than life. Alec is puzzled by this remark, but the reader is not. To embrace life fully, with all its ups and downs, and to risk hurt as well as joy by entering into a relationship with another person, takes a certain sort of bravery.

Frederick does not believe that Alec possesses this kind of courage. He is wrong. Alec ultimately risks everything for the one person he loves, showing a bravery of a sort his father would not have expected and his mother would not have understood.

Victim of his parents' unhappy marriage

Alec is an unwitting pawn in his parents' 'terrible game'. Alicia uses Alec to shield her from the necessity of ever being alone with her husband. This means that Alec is denied the chance to go away to school and to meet boys his own age. When Alicia realises that Alec will never be a good companion to her, she does not hesitate to sacrifice him by insisting that he join the army in order to hurt her husband and to allow her some vicarious glory.

No interest in women

There can be little doubt that Alicia's controlling, domineering manner and his parents' unhappy marriage leaves Alec emotionally scarred. One result of this is that he is not particularly interested in relationships or women. Jerry is very curious and dearly wants to sleep with a woman, but Alec says that he has only a 'mild curiosity, well contained'.

Ineffectual

Although it is cruel of Alec's mother to say it, there is no doubt that Alec is an ineffectual man. Neither his superior officers nor the enlisted men in his charge respect him. Sergeant Barry holds Alec in thinly-veiled contempt and even the men who do like him talk to him in an informal, vaguely disrespectful way. The first time Bennett arranges a horse riding excursion, Alec asks Jerry's commanding officer if he can 'have Private Crowe for an hour or so'. The breezy reply: 'You can and welcome,' strikes Alec as mildly insolent. He says that the man would 'never have spoken like that to the major or indeed Bennett'.

Alec is very like his father in many ways. Alicia claims that Frederick is not Alec's biological father, and we never learn if this is, in fact, the case. But whether it is genetics or upbringing, Alec does grow more and more like Frederick Moore over the years. Alicia notices this and she is disgusted by it. On the night before Alec leaves to join the army, Alicia refers to the similarity between Alec and Frederick, telling her son accusingly that he is 'growing more and more like him every day'.

Cautious and rather timid

Alec is so used to being an observer rather than a participant that he finds it difficult to act quickly or decisively. When he meets Jerry for the first time, Alec does not immediately respond to Jerry's invitation to join him in the lake. Instead, he thinks about it for a short while before stripping off his clothes and swimming out to the other boy.

'I have always been cautious'

When Jerry offers him a drink of poteen to toast his new horse, Alec is suspicious and admits: 'I have always been cautious.' This natural caution means, of course, that Alec has no interest in going to fight in the war. Alicia berates him for his cowardice, and although Alec does not like the word, he does not argue.

It is ironic that Alicia's controlling, domineering nature should be part of the reason for Alec growing into the sort of timid man that she despises. She snaps her fingers at him as if he were a dog, speaks to him in a tone that will brook no argument, and renders her son incapable of standing up for himself. It is not surprising, therefore, that Alec should grow into a young man who blushes easily and goes along with his parents' plans for him, even when he disagrees with them. When Alicia tells him about her intention to bring him to Europe with her, Alec wonders aloud what would happen if he were to refuse to go. Alicia says that he won't refuse, and he replies, 'No. I don't suppose I will.'

Finds it difficult to express emotion

Alec has difficulty in expressing or even understanding emotion. The coldness and hostility of his parents' marriage scars him and leaves him virtually unable to recognise or properly identify different emotions, let alone express his own emotions in an appropriate way. Jerry is the only person with whom Alec seems truly comfortable. Jerry alone manages to break through Alec's protective exterior and find a place in his heart. In all his dealings with others, Alec is compliant and obedient in general, and he is never the initiator. With Jerry, things are different. Alec seeks out his friend whenever he gets the chance, even when this means risking a reprimand from his commanding officer. It is his love for Jerry which ultimately leads Alec to make the bravest and most catastrophic decision of his life.

Gentle, thoughtful and kind

Alec may have difficulty expressing emotion but that is not to say that he does not feel any emotion. He is a kind, thoughtful young man who dislikes causing others pain. At the start of the novel, he regrets distressing the army chaplain with his frivolity and refusal to repent and seek comfort in faith and prayer.

> The enlisted men like Alec too, but they do not fear him and they do not treat him with a great deal of respect

Alec's gentleness attracts Bennett, who admits that he had never thought he would admire such a trait in another man. The enlisted men like Alec too, but they do not fear him and they do not treat him with a great deal of respect. Bennett points out that though the men like the fact that Alec is 'fair and decent and kind to them', they would not follow him into battle. Like his father, Alec does not possess the ability to command authority.

Class conscious

Alec comes from a wealthy and privileged family but he sees his social position as an obstacle, not a benefit. He says that as a child he was 'isolated from the surrounding children of my own age by the traditional barriers of class'. Like Frederick, who tells Alec that Alicia may be right when she says that he is 'a peasant at heart', Alec sees little positive about the wealth and privilege that go with being one of the landed gentry. He is happiest when he is with Jerry and he does not care in the slightest that Jerry is from a poor, village family.

One of the tragedies in Alec's life is that he does not belong anywhere. He does not fit in with those of his own class because their values do not matter to him, and neither does he blend in with the villagers in Wicklow or the enlisted men in the army. Wherever he is, Alec seems to find difficulty fitting in. Although he is born into privilege, he is not a typical member of the Ascendancy, that is, the wealthy, Protestant upper class. He can act the part if necessary, and he is as 'charming and detached' as all the other people of his class that he and his mother meet on their trip to Europe, but he has no interest in this life. His distaste for it is shown in the cursory treatment given to his time in Europe, a mere paragraph, compared to his detailed descriptions of his time with Jerry.

Final impression

Alec has nothing left to live for, and he faces the idea of his impending execution with equanimity, telling the army chaplain that he shall 'sing gladly' as he goes to meet his maker. This ready acceptance of death is heartbreaking, although perhaps death is less frightening to Alec than life. Alec is a young man damaged and scarred by self-absorbed parents and the tragic ending of his only foray into a close relationship with another person. Although we may mourn Alec's fate, we cannot help but feel that, had he lived, his life would have been a barren, unfulfilled one.

Jerry Crowe

First impression

Alec and Jerry first speak in early May. Alec finds Jerry swimming in the Moores' private lake but Jerry seems completely unfazed at being caught trespassing. He calls Alec to join him and reacts with contempt to Alec's asking him if he knows he is on private property. Rules do not appear to mean much to Jerry.

It is obvious that Jerry is not in the least intimidated by Alec's superior social position. He sees himself as Alec's equal and strikes a bargain with him: Jerry will teach Alec to fight if Alec teaches him to ride. Jerry is relaxed and very much in charge in this first conversation with Alec.

Keenly aware of class differences

From an early age Jerry is more alive to the class differences between himself and Alec than Alec is. It is Jerry who points out to Alec that neither family would tolerate a friendship between the pair.

Jerry may recognise the problems of befriending someone from a different social class but that does not mean that he accepts the situation without any resentment. When he and Alec meet at the point-to-point, they have not seen each other for some time, and Jerry seems more distant with his old friend than at any time in the past. The situation is awkward: Alec's father is presenting the prize and Jerry's role, to a certain extent, is that of a grateful underling. He is even wearing a pair of Alec's cast-off breeches. Jerry does not catch Alec's eye and, when Alec congratulates him, calls him 'sir'. Alec's open, friendly manner breaks through Jerry's reserve in this instance, but before the pair can really have a conversation, Alec's mother drags him away.

It is Jerry who first points out that when they both join the army, Alec will be made an officer and will travel first-class on the train to Belfast. Jerry realises that the commanding officers will be unhappy with an officer being friendly with an enlisted man and, once they are serving soldiers, Jerry is careful not to be seen to talk to Alec too much.

Loyal friend

It would be easy to say that a person in Jerry's position would want to be friendly with someone from a higher social class, but the truth is that Jerry does not benefit from Alec's wealth or status at all. At no stage does Jerry presume on the friendship. He doesn't take the job Alec offers to find for him in the Moores' stables because he knows it would make their friendship impossible. When his father goes missing in action and Alec offers to help Jerry's family financially, Jerry also refuses.

Because Jerry is an enlisted man and Alec is an officer, it is difficult for them to find time to talk to one another. However, when they do, the strength of their affection for one another is clear. Jerry even takes off Alec's boots and tries to ease the pain in his swollen feet by rubbing alcohol into them. Jerry is unwell too, but he puts Alec's comfort above his own, saying that he finds it easier to cope with pain than Alec does. This is unlikely to be true and, indeed, Alec says that 'the illness in his eyes as he smiled at me was a reflection of my own'.

> Unlike Alec, Jerry does not have the luxury of a long childhood. He has to leave school at a young age and go to work to help support his family

Forced to grow up quickly

Unlike Alec, Jerry does not have the luxury of a long childhood. He has to leave school at a young age and go to work to help support his family.

Jerry gets a job as a farm labourer and that hastens his transition from childhood to adulthood. He begins smoking and adopting the mannerisms of older men. Alec notices the change and says that Jerry 'no longer seemed to be a child'. When Alec coughs and splutters on one of Jerry's borrowed cigarettes, Jerry laughs and looks 'immensely superior and old, old as a tree'.

While Jerry affects the habits of grown men, he does not have as much experience of life as he would like others to believe. To celebrate the acquisition of his first horse, Jerry toasts her with poteen. He offers Alec a drink too, saying that it is 'man's stuff' and that it will make hairs grow on Alec's chest. The strong alcohol is too much for Alec and, for all his talk, too much for Jerry as well. In Alec's company, Jerry can drop the facade of manhood for a while and he admits to Alec that he has never actually had poteen before.

'The Germans are going to fix all those eejits in Europe, the British are going to fix the Germans'

Much of Jerry's adult behaviour is faked. He talks about the coming war as if he knows all about it, but his language is still childish and his views simplistic: 'The Germans are going to fix all those eejits in Europe, the British are going to fix the Germans.'

It is not just in the matter of politics that Jerry acts older than his years. Although he has never been with a woman, he has strong views on the nature of women. He says that women want more than men can give and that Alec's mother wants more than all of them. Alec observes that Jerry sounds as if he were 'older than the hills' and Jerry replies that he was born old and never got any younger.

Proud of his country/nationalistic

Jerry is steeped in Irish culture. Even when he plays the mouth organ, which he plays 'with great virtuosity', Jerry reflects Irish culture and history. He plays sentimental or revolutionary ballads alongside 'ancient wordless tunes'.

Jerry's republican sympathies surface early in the novel when he tells Alec that 'we are going to fix the British'. While he is undoubtedly parroting the words of older men, his allegiance is clear.

As Jerry grows older, his views become more fully formed. The night before they leave to join the army, Jerry reacts strongly to Alec's casual comment about Jerry being 'with the Shinners'. He realises, even if Alec doesn't, that this is a serious matter and that a violent conflict in Ireland is likely to happen soon.

Jerry's dream of a free Ireland stays with him until the very end. Indeed, he dies with the words of the revolutionary song 'The Croppy Boy' on his lips.

Loyal son

Neither of Jerry's parents appear to be particularly good parents. On the night before he enlists, Jerry tells Alec that his father is 'rare and quick with the fist and you need to be always showing him a brave face'. Jerry's mother is little better. She is keen for Jerry to join the army so that he, like his father, can earn a soldier's wage and help support the family.

When Mrs Crowe writes to Jerry to say his father is missing in action, Jerry's first reaction is to find his father. This is despite the fact that all his mother seems to want is certainty so that she can either continue to get her husband's wages or his pension.

> Jerry's dream of a free Ireland stays with him until the very end. Indeed, he dies with the words of the revolutionary song 'The Croppy Boy' on his lips

Jerry's determination to help his mother leads to his undoing. Major Glendinning has made it clear from the start that he will punish deserters with court-martial and execution, a fact of which Jerry would have been well aware before he left. He is unrepentant, however, telling Alec that if he had the chance, he'd do it again.

Kind and humane

Jerry may be a soldier and he may wish to continue fighting when he gets home to Ireland, but he does not enjoy the suffering of others. Even when Bennett idly remarks that he hopes the major, who threatens to report them for taking horses, is killed by a stray bullet, Jerry can't agree. He says that he would not wish such an end on his worst enemy. Equally, he is very distressed by the dreadful conditions in which the horses are kept at the front, and he wants to do something to help them. Naturally, he is appalled by the screaming of the dying man in No-Man's Land, and he tells Alec that he did his best to shoot the man and end his misery but was unable to see him clearly enough to get a proper aim.

Cynical and pragmatic

Jerry goes along with Alec's dream of sharing ownership of a racing yard some day but he is aware that the dream is unlikely ever to become a reality. Jerry knows that his future is more or less mapped out for him and that his social class limits his options. He knows, for example, that if he were to work for Alec's father, it would be impossible for Alec and he to remain friends. Jerry sees the world more clearly than Alec does and he knows that he is surrounded by people who want him to do things that will suit them, rather than things that will be good for him. For example, his mother wants him to join the army, like his father, so that she will have double pay arriving by post.

> Jerry sees the world more clearly than Alec does and he knows that he is surrounded by people who want him to do things that will suit them, rather than things that will be good for him

Perhaps it is his knowledge of his own mother's nature that makes Jerry better able to understand Alec's mother than Alec himself does. He wonders if the story about Frederick Moore not being Alec's father is true, and when Alec appears astonished that he should even ask such a question, Jerry replies, 'You're the one they'll make an officer out of.' He is slightly contemptuous of Alec's naivety and says that people 'say what suits them' in order to get their own way.

No interest in the outcome of the war

Jerry makes it clear from the start that he is in the army for two reasons: to make money and to train as a soldier so that he can play an important role in the inevitable fight for Irish independence. When Bennett takes him and Alec to a vantage point from which they can see the battlefield around Ypres, Jerry is unimpressed. Unlike Bennett, who wishes he could be involved, Jerry says that he'd 'rather watch it than be in it' and that he'd 'rather be at home than either'.

Final impression

Jerry Crowe is a kind, decent, humane young man whose misfortune it is to be in the power of people who view him as expendable. As a boy, he is expected to leave school early to help support his family. As a young man he is encouraged to join the army to earn even more money for his mother. And as a soldier he is expected to be part of the war machine and to do exactly as he is told. His own needs are not taken into consideration at all.

Jerry is a good friend to Alec and the one bright light in the other young man's life. It is understandable that, without him, Alec sees no point in carrying on.

 # Alicia Moore

First impression

Our interest in Alicia Moore is aroused in the opening paragraphs when Alec, considering his parents' reaction to the news of his execution, says that his 'heart doesn't bleed' for his mother. This is an unusual sentiment for a son and we wonder what it is about his mother that has led Alec to feel so bitter towards her.

Selfish and intolerant

When Alec describes his lonely, mostly loveless childhood in Wicklow we soon learn why he dislikes his mother so much.

The incident with Alec's piano teacher is our first real insight into Alicia's character. She is impatient with her son's lack of progress at the instrument and contemptuous of his piano tutor, a timid man who is unnerved by both Alicia's beauty and her haughty manner. The tutor is fired and Alicia begins to teach Alec the piano herself. However, her selfishness and impatience mean that she soon becomes bored with the piano lessons and so she ends Alec's musical education abruptly.

It is not only the piano teacher who comments on Alicia's beauty. On the night before he leaves to enlist, Jerry tells Alec that Alicia is very beautiful and he compares her to Helen of Troy. This is an appropriate comparison; Helen of Troy is famous as the woman whose beauty 'launched a thousand ships' and caused two nations to go to war over her. Alicia is sending her son to war to fight and possibly die for her. Alicia's physical beauty contrasts sharply with the ugliness of her soul.

Class conscious

It is not only in her dealings with the piano tutor that Alicia shows her snobbery, she is horrified when she hears of Alec's friendship with Jerry. She speaks dismissively of Jerry, seeming to find it difficult to find the right words to describe him. She settles on calling him a child from the village and tells Alec that he must stop seeing his friend as it is not *'comme il faut'* (the done thing).

On another occasion, Alec tells his parents that he has heard there will be a war, and Alicia asks where he got such an idea. She is horrified to think that he might have been chatting to the servants and her voice rises 'to a slight gasp at the thought'.

When Alec and Jerry meet at the point-to-point, Alec is as eager as ever to chat to his old friend. Alicia insists that Alec take her home immediately and pulls him away from Jerry. As they travel home in the car, Alicia says that Jerry is more than likely involved with some criminal organisation. She says darkly that you 'never can tell what those sort of people will get up to'. When Alec tries to argue, she reverts to French again, *'Parlons d'autre choses.'* Her use of French in this case is slightly affected and unnecessary and is clearly just another way for her to show that she is a member of the upper class. It is significant that the more emotionally charged the conversation, the more Alicia retreats behind French phrases. It is as if social position and the trappings of the upper class are a shield against the more unpleasant realities of life. To Alicia, the most important thing is appearances. As Alec remarks to Jerry on the eve of their departure: 'My mother thinks if we don't dress for dinner the world'll fall apart.'

> To Alicia, the most important thing is appearances. As Alec remarks to Jerry on the eve of their departure: 'My mother thinks if we don't dress for dinner the world'll fall apart'

Lacks maternal instinct – cruel and manipulative

Alicia Moore has little regard for her son's feelings or his needs. She uses him to shield her from the necessity of having to be alone with her husband, whom she detests. Even at a young age, Alec realises that his mother views him as little more than a pawn in 'some terrible game'.

To Alicia, Alec is little more than a toy to be used for her amusement. She tells him that she wants to bring him with her to Europe as he is now 'old enough to be a good companion'. She wants her son to take care of her but she shows no interest in his upbringing or education beyond those areas which impact on her.

By far the most chilling demonstration of Alicia's lack of any motherly feeling is shown in the conversation she has with Alec the night before he leaves to join the army. It is clear that Alicia wants to be the mother of a brave hero and to bask in the reflected glory of her soldier son. That she doesn't care if Alec is killed in the war is quite obvious; her desire to send him off to fight seems to stem from her witnessing the drama surrounding the death of Christopher Boyle. She says she was there when the telegram came, and Alec describes her expression as 'strangely excited' when she tells her husband and son the news. It seems unthinkable that a mother could be willing to risk her only son's life in order to bring her some attention.

> It is clear that Alicia wants to be the mother of a brave hero and to bask in the reflected glory of her soldier son. That she doesn't care if Alec is killed in the war is quite obvious

Alec maintains that he does not want to fight for a cause he doesn't understand and doesn't care about. His mother pours scorn on him, calling him a coward and saying that he is just like his father. Alec apologises for being 'inadequate'. Alicia unkindly agrees that the word describes him well.

Alec stands up to his mother's criticism and seems unmoved by her cruelty and scorn. This is hardly surprising as he has grown up with such treatment and is used to it. Realising this, Alicia plays her trump card. In an act of almost unspeakable cruelty, she tells Alec that Frederick is not his father. This news crushes her son but Alicia doesn't care how upset he is. She has achieved her aim, which was to sever the connection between Alec and her husband. Now Alec feels he has nothing to live for, so is willing to join the army and go to war.

It is hard to imagine a mother sinking to these depths to get her own way but it is clear that Alicia Moore is devoid of any feelings of maternal love for her son. When Alec announces the following morning that he is leaving to join the army immediately, Alicia pretends to protest a little, but Alec says that in spite of her words he was 'conscious of a radiance coming from her, a feeling of triumph'. Alec describes her standing in the drawing room and throwing her arms out 'with a splendidly theatrical gesture' when he walks in. Her eyes, he says, are 'the most triumphant blue'. Alicia never once expresses any concern for Alec's well-being, all she cares about is that she gets to see him in his uniform (he deprives her of this pleasure) and that she receives letters regularly.

Alicia writes to Alec but her letter contains no hint of concern for him. She says she is 'wounded' by Alec's lack of correspondence. There is nothing loving or maternal in her letter, and it is clear that Alec's departure has not distressed her at all.

Cruel to her husband

Alicia holds her husband in utter contempt and makes no attempt to hide the fact. When Frederick suggests sending Alec away to school, Alicia reminds him of an agreement that he made years ago to keep the boy at home. She says that she has 'no intention of remaining alone in this house' with her husband. That she says this in front of her son adds to the cruelty of her words.

Alicia's detestation of her husband is evident in all her dealings with him. She scorns him and belittles him at every opportunity and seems to delight in his misery. At her command, Frederick advises Alec against continuing his friendship with Jerry. His rather vague and gentle approach does not impress Alicia and she tells her husband that he never speaks 'with authority'. She goes on to accuse him of having 'always been an ineffective man'. Frederick makes no effort to defend himself, though he is clearly distressed by her words, but she continues to stick the knife in the wound by adding that he is not only ineffective but old as well.

We really see when she determines to send Alec off to war how monstrously cruel Alicia can be to her husband. Frederick becomes distressed every time the subject of the war is brought up, and this seems to give Alicia pleasure. Alec recounts how he storms out of the room one day, shouting that the young men who join up are merely 'food for cannons'. Far from being concerned at her husband's distress, Alicia merely smiles.

The way Alicia breaks the news of her decision to force Alec to join up is typically cruel. She appears to show a solicitous interest in Frederick, saying that he appears unwell and should perhaps go to see the doctor. Her real motive in advising her husband to take better care of himself soon becomes clear when she says that once Alec is gone to war, Frederick 'won't have him to rely on'. Frederick and Alec laugh at the suggestion that Alec will become a soldier, but Alicia is deadly serious. When Frederick realises this, he begs Alicia not to take away his son. She scorns him for his weakness and repeatedly tells him that he is old. Alec will go to war. Alicia will have her way.

Charming in public but hides her true nature

Alec describes his mother as possessing 'a contrived radiance which strangers took for reality, but which seemed to me to be a thin shell covering some black burning rage which constantly consumed her'.

Bitter and resentful

Alicia Moore is a deeply unhappy woman who is determined to make those around her share in her misery. Whenever she sees a sign that Alec or Frederick might be happy, she feels the need to destroy their contentment.

It is this bitter determination to ruin the happiness of others that is partly responsible for Alicia's insistence on Alec going to war. She sees that both Alec and his father are enjoying an increasingly close relationship from which she is excluded. Ironically, it was her insistence that Alec end his friendship with Jerry which led to this bond between father and son.

Alicia's hatred for her husband and for the life she feels she has been forced into leads her to behave monstrously to the people closest to her. On the night before he leaves to join the army, she tells Alec that she only married his father because she was already pregnant with another man's child. We are never sure if the story she tells Alec is true or not; Alicia Moore appears to be a woman who is perfectly capable of inventing such a tale if it will further her ends.

Final impression

Alicia Moore is a cold, calculating, evil, completely unredeemed woman. She never once shows any hint of kindness or love and seems utterly indifferent to the needs of those around her. She is a shockingly cruel person and by the end of the book we completely understand Alec's lack of interest in her reaction to the news of his execution.

Frederick Moore

First impression

Our first impression of Frederick Moore is that he is a weak man who is unable to stand up to his domineering and manipulative wife.

Frederick's marriage to Alicia is an unhappy one. His wife despises him and makes no effort to hide the fact from him or from their son.

Alec's father does try to do his best for his son but there is a sense in which he views the boy as Alicia's property. When Frederick suggests sending Alec to school, Alicia swiftly reminds him that he agreed long ago that she could keep the boy at home as she has 'no intention of remaining alone in this house' with her husband. Frederick is incapable of standing up to her icy determination. Alicia possesses far more strength of character than her husband and even Frederick himself seems unconvinced by his own arguments. Alec describes him as speaking 'without any enormous conviction' when he tells his son of the benefits of school. Indeed, it would be hard for Frederick to argue convincingly that school is the best way to achieve success in life as he is clearly not happy in his own life despite being sent away to school when he was a young boy.

It is kindness and affection that prompts Frederick to suggest Alec be sent to school. He realises the boy is lonely and knows that it is important for him to 'meet a few chaps' of his own age. However, even though the offer was well-intentioned, Alec's father's fear of Alicia's displeasure is stronger than his desire to do the right thing by his son.

Lonely and unhappy

His deep unhappiness leads Frederick Moore to withdraw into himself. He busies himself with 'farm matters' and spends his free time reading or 'working at his pipe'. This retreat from his family means that Frederick never gives his full attention to any conversation going on around him. His dealings with his son are stilted and awkward, though well-meaning. When he first tackles Alec about his friendship with Jerry, we get the impression that it is Alicia who has forced him to talk to his son about the matter. She wants to take Alec with her to Europe and all the evidence in the book so far suggests that she will have her way. Frederick broaches the topic in the drawing room after dinner and his discomfort is obvious. He fiddles with his pipe and avoids meeting his son's eye. When he does speak, there is a sense that he is parroting Alicia's words. He says, 'We think it's time you stretched your wings a bit,' but he almost immediately asks Alec if he approves of this plan to go to Europe. Alicia is angry with the question and Frederick does not press the matter. Instead, he asks Alec if he would like to help him with the hunt and with the work on the estate. He is making an effort to connect with his son in the only way he knows how, but even this level of interaction embarrasses Alec. Frederick's forced jollity when he says 'perhaps the time has come for us to get to know each other better' is about as personal as he has ever been in his conversations with his son, and we get the impression that neither of them are quite sure how to handle this relatively intimate chat.

'Perhaps the time has come for us to get to know each other better'

Frederick Moore only becomes truly animated when talking of his love for the land. When he is instructing Alec in the management of the estate, he tells the boy how important it is to treat the land well. He describes it as if it were a woman, saying: 'To love the land is more rewarding than any ...' He trails off, embarrassed, but it is clear that he was about to say that his relationship with the land is more rewarding than his relationships with other people.

Although Alec and Frederick become closer when they work together on estate business, Alec says that his father seems to be glad of his company 'in the same sort of way that a man on a desert island must be glad to see and talk to his own shadow from time to time'.

Has little to live for

There is a sense in which Frederick Moore has given up on life and on his family in particular. He knows his wife hates him and there is little he can do about it. He tells Alec that 'where I can have no possible influence a terrible lethargy sets in'. He regrets this but we feel that he does not now see any way in which he can improve the situation. He does his wife's bidding, not because he agrees with her, but because he has neither the strength nor the will to stand up to her. It is easier to let her have her own way, and this is what Frederick does.

> Sadly, it is not only his own life which is being ruined by his dreadful relationship with his wife, it is Alec's too

Sadly, it is not only his own life which is being ruined by his dreadful relationship with his wife, it is Alec's too.

Frederick is an ineffectual man. Alicia is cruel when she describes him as lacking in authority and says that he is an 'ineffective man' but there is more than a grain of truth in what she says. However, his wife's obvious scorn and contempt does little to boost Frederick's self-esteem or make him a more confident husband and father. Alicia cruelly calls him 'ineffective and old' and he does not bother to argue with her.

Finds it difficult to express his emotions

Because of his own upbringing and his social background, Frederick Moore is not comfortable when it comes to emotions. He does love his son but finds it next to impossible to express this love openly. Instead, he resorts to material displays of affection. He buys Alec a beautiful, expensive mare and Alec's delight pleases his father. The ultimate example of this use of objects to demonstrate feeling is shown on the morning of Alec's departure for the front. Frederick does his best to hide his heartbreak at the thought of his son leaving and confines his conversation to rather matter-of-fact topics such as whether or not Alec has enough money, and what he will do with Alec's mare in his absence. However, his hands are shaking as he picks up the newspaper and it is obvious that he is wrestling with some strong emotion. Unable or unwilling to articulate his love and concern for his son, Frederick gives Alec a gold watch, calling it 'a traditional gesture' as he acknowledges that 'sentimentality' doesn't suit either of them. Alec and his father part ways with a minimum of fuss but with clear love on both sides. This contrasts strongly with Alicia's theatrical, superficial behaviour in the drawing room moments later when she gleefully says goodbye to her son.

Locked in a loveless marriage

Frederick Moore tells Alec that he feels it is partly Alicia's beauty which has led her to become such a bitter, unhappy woman. He says that it must be 'a terrible thing' to be a beautiful woman and to 'always expect people to die for you'. He also points out that beautiful people know their beauty will not last forever and that the power they wield will diminish as their looks fade. The thought of Alicia facing the prospect of 'wrinkled fingers' and 'no one left to die for her' gives Frederick a sort of grim pleasure.

Final impression

Frederick Moore is a kind, well-meaning, weak man. He is locked in an unhappy marriage, and although he loves his son, he does not have the emotional vocabulary to express his love. Like Alec, Frederick sees his life as being largely outside his control. What he can do, he does. He keeps the land on the estate in good order but knows that it will be handed back to the Irish (from whom it was taken) before long. Frederick's life is a lonely one. There is a glimmer of hope and happiness when Alec starts to work with him on estate business, but Alicia cruelly puts a stop to this by sending Alec off to war.

In the opening paragraphs of the novel, Alec remarks that the news of his impending death may kill his father, but he also notes that Frederick Moore 'may be better off dead'. Such a sentiment may seem heartless until we see the lonely misery that is life in the Moore household.

Major Glendinning

First impressions

Our first impressions of Major Glendinning are that he is a tough, unsympathetic man. He speaks contemptuously of the Irish men he has been assigned, calling them 'illiterate peasants, rascals and schoolboys'. He is determined to turn them into soldiers as quickly and efficiently as possible but he despises their lack of professional soldiering spirit.

Understands his men

However, it soon emerges that the major has a certain understanding of the men in his charge. For example, he notices that Alec does not mix well with the other officers and holds himself somewhat aloof from them. His comment, 'I watch, you know' is telling, as it becomes clear later on that he does indeed watch and has a better insight into the soldiers' lives than they might think. He disapproves of Alec's friendship with Jerry, seeing that it has the potential to weaken discipline in the ranks.

A soldier, first and foremost

Major Glendinning's primary concern is the outcome of the war. His sole aim is to provide the army with the soldiers it needs. When he is telling Alec about an upcoming attack, he says that 'there must be no flaw in the machinery'. He says that to him and to the War Office, the soldiers are not men: they are simply part of the war machine. He does not question the need for war, nor does he question the orders he carries out.

Anti-Irish

The major knows that there are those among the Irish recruits who are in favour of Irish independence and he is deeply suspicious of such men. He is concerned lest they change sides during the war and give the Germans vital intelligence. In his eyes, Irish soldiers cannot be trusted. He asks Alec if he too is 'tainted with the Irish disease' of disloyalty and disaffection.

Major Glendinning believes that the Irish are an overly-emotional race and that this makes them unfit to govern themselves. He blames Alec's Irishness for the fact that he is friendly with Jerry and his refusal to take his advice on the subject of men and officers fraternising.

Mirror image of Alicia Moore

Alec flees the unbearable situation at home and his mother's cruel, controlling influence only to land himself in an almost identical situation, but with higher stakes. Major Glendinning shares Alicia's contempt for the peasant Irish and he too wants to make a man of Alec and separate him from Jerry Crowe.

Major Glendinning's habits are startlingly similar to those of Alicia Moore. The major clings rigidly to the mannerisms of polite society, even going so far as to bring a lemon with him to the front in order that he might be able to slice it into his tea. It seems an oddly pointless act in the middle of the horror and death that is the front line but, like Alicia, Major Glendinning likes to keep up the appearance and habits of the upper class.

> Major Glendinning shares Alicia's contempt for the peasant Irish and he too wants to make a man of Alec and separate him from Jerry Crowe

Traces of compassion/a complex character

Major Glendinning is not without compassion, though he hides it well. He offers Alec the opportunity to visit his family when they are passing through Dublin, having noted that the Moores live reasonably close by.

The major does his best to bring Alec around to his way of thinking and takes quite an interest in the young officer. In his own way, he is trying to help Alec by toughening him up and making him more like a typical soldier.

Major Glendinning believes that in order for a war to be fought successfully, the soldiers must be viewed as part of the machine and not as individuals. However, though he may act this way and may try his best to persuade Alec to see things the same way, the major does know that the men in his charge have lives and worries and families of their own. When Alec requests compassionate leave for Jerry, Major Glendinning refuses, but asks Alec if he has thought about 'how many men in the British Expeditionary Force have fathers, brothers, sons, cousins missing, wounded, dead'.

An incident which shows all the facets of Major Glendinning's character occurs shortly after he returns to the front and hears the screams of the dying soldier in No Man's Land. The man has been lying there for four days by the time the major returns to the trenches, but nobody has done anything about it. Major Glendinning acts quickly and decisively and takes Alec with him to see what can be done about the situation. His bravery and compassion are clearly shown here, in that he is risking his own life to put the dying soldier out of his misery.

> *'how many men in the British Expeditionary Force have fathers, brothers, sons, cousins missing, wounded, dead'*

Although the major's decision to help the soldier from the Gloucesters is a compassionate and brave one, his refusal to do so until he has finished writing his report might be viewed as callous and uncaring. However, it is not as heartless as it might first appear. Major Glendinning is a soldier first and foremost and never neglects his duty. If he is going to risk death to help another man, then he ensures that his affairs are in order and that his last report is completed. He deliberately suppresses any emotion he might feel on listening to the dying man's tortured screams and refers to the hazardous journey into No Man's Land as 'an outing' to 'see to him'. His language is brisk and matter-of-fact and he does his best to hide any emotion he might feel. Nevertheless, he does swear aloud when he sees the man's injuries and sighs 'a long sad sigh' as the screaming stops.

Decisive

It may be argued that by killing the wounded soldier the major is acting cruelly, but he is left with little choice. He does not set out with the intention of ending the man's life but he knows it is the most likely outcome. He brings Alec with him and presumably they would have carried the man back to the trenches if there were any hope of saving his life. Before they go, he tells Alec that 'we can make no decisions until we make ourselves fully aware of the situation'. It falls to the major to make the difficult decision when he sees the extent of the man's injuries, and he does not flinch from doing so.

Dehumanised by soldiering/war

It is easy to view Major Glendinning as a cruel, heartless man but he is a product of the career he has chosen. The war has forced him to make harsh decisions about the men in his charge. In a way, he is as much a victim of the war as Jerry and Alec. He has been forced to subjugate his own humanity and to become a ruthless, efficient soldier. Although he is a professional soldier, the horrors of the First World War and the scale of the human losses are unlike anything he would have experienced before.

In his first description of Major Glendinning, Alec notes that the major 'looked like a man who knew all about self-control'. Alec's insubordination and his insistence on viewing Jerry as a friend and not just another enlisted man disturbs Major Glendinning, partly because Alec is giving rein to a side of himself that the major has deliberately and determinedly suppressed. He tries to teach Alec to behave the same way, assuring him that he will be better off when he too can view the men as little more than cattle. Alec's stubborn refusal to act unemotionally threatens the major's own ability to keep his feelings firmly in check. This can be seen in the last pages of the novel when

Jerry is arrested for going absent without leave. Once again, Major Glendinning attempts to impress on Alec the necessity of putting his loyalty to the army above his loyalty to his friend. When Alec calls the British army uniform 'some sort of fancy dress', Major Gendinning's reaction is an emotional one. He pales, strikes Alec across the face with his cane, and sits down again, hands trembling. It is clear that Alec has the ability to get under the major's skin and cause him to lose his famous self-control.

> He has not managed to 'make a man' of Alec, and Alec's emotional response to Jerry's sentence is just the type of thing the major despises

In the opening pages of the novel, Alec notes that Major Glendinning has not been to see him since his arrest. It would appear that the major has finally conceded that his efforts to turn Alec into an officer in his own mould have failed completely. He has not managed to 'make a man' of Alec, and Alec's emotional response to Jerry's sentence is just the type of thing the major despises. As the major is not the type to tolerate failure or weakness, it is safe to say that he would have no further interest in Alec, nor would he wish to speak to him before his execution.

Final impression

Our final impression of Major Glendinning is of a determined, inflexible man who has thrown himself wholeheartedly into the war effort and has decided that the best way to achieve success is not to question orders from those in a position of authority, but to follow such orders to the letter. Naturally, he wants his junior officers and his men to have the same attitude and he cannot and does not tolerate any deviation from this chain of command. Major Glendinning's putting Alec in charge of the firing squad may be viewed as an extremely cruel act, but it may also be seen as an attempt to force Alec to face up to his responsibilities as an officer. Major Glendinning himself does not flinch from such tasks. The major may have traces of compassion but he works hard to suppress any feelings which may lead him to have sympathy with his men and see them as individuals rather than as part of the war machine.

Officer on a night-time trench inspection

 *Bennett*

First impressions

Bennett, another junior officer, is English, and even though he is roughly the same age as Alec and just as inexperienced, he has 'the air of someone who had seen it all before'. He and Alec share a small attic at West Outre and a dug-out at the front line, and come to know one another reasonably well.

Adventurous and dashing – ready to break rules when necessary

Bennett has little time for rules and regulations. Bored at the farmhouse in West Outre, he arranges for himself and Alec to go horse riding. He dismisses Alec's concerns about Major Glendinning's reaction with a cool: 'Who's going to tell him?'

It is never clear how exactly Bennett gets hold of the horses for their excursions but Jerry and Alec suspect that he 'pinched them'. This 'healthy disrespect for authority' as Bennett calls it, is, he claims, a result of his time at public school. It seems that he regards the war as simply an extension of his boarding school days in some ways.

Bennett's sense of adventure leads him to wish for some action. On their first horse-riding excursion, he takes Alec and Jerry to the top of a hill to see what he calls his 'show'. It is the battleground of Ypres, stretching far below them. All that can be seen is fire, smoke and what Alec describes as a 'grey tormented landscape'. Alec observes that there is no sign of life in this appalling place. The scene seems horrifying but Bennett is almost enchanted by it and wishes to be in the thick of the battle. The idea of being a hero thrills him.

Bennett's disregard for authority threatens to get him into trouble but he manages to avoid punishment for his transgressions. When the 'small irate major' questions Bennett and his companions as they ride back to base after their first trek, Bennett seems almost to delight in angering the man further. When the major wants to know who they are so he can report them to their commanding officer, Bennett flippantly adds that he thinks the Royal Irish Rifles, to which he is attached, 'apparently have a shortage of junior officers'.

Escaping a dull life and keen to seek excitement

Bennett claims that his life to date has been 'indescribably dull'. Everything, he says, has been predictable and boring. The war is something new. Bennett tells Alec that he will 'either become a hero' or die. He seems excited at the prospect, saying that death 'is a mystery'. He is surprised that neither Jerry nor Alec seem keen on the prospect of doing something in battle that might 'stir the blood'. When the men come under heavy fire at the front some time later, Bennett is delighted. While the men around him are sickened and numbed by the slaughter, Bennett jokes and laughs and his eyes sparkle with excitement.

> Bennett tells Alec that he will 'either become a hero' or die. He seems excited at the prospect, saying that death 'is a mystery'

Alec is not entirely comfortable with Bennett's love of danger and his desire to push the boundaries. He recognises in his fellow officer 'the sort of man who would always push his luck'. This is not Alec's way at all, although, ironically, he ends up being the one who breaks the rules far more than Bennett has ever done.

Detached, cynical and worldly wise

Part of Bennett's desire to fight may be attributed to his detachment. He refers to the war as 'this show' as if it were a play in which he was acting. He does not value human life as highly as Alec or Jerry. When the 'small irate major' threatens to report Bennett and his companions for taking horses and riding out for pleasure, Bennett hopes that the man will be killed by a stray bullet. Jerry says that he wouldn't wish such an end on anyone but Bennett responds that it is unwise 'to be squeamish about such things'.

Bennett epitomises some of what Major Glendinning feels are the necessary qualities for an officer. He may question authority, something on which he prides himself, but Alec notes that 'he never really cared what the answer was, it only seemed important to him that he should ask the question'. He is quite detached, and although he is polite and friendly, there is always a sense that he is not particularly concerned about the individual men under his command. Indeed, he tells Alec that he intends to become more like Major Glendinning in order to get the men to obey him unquestioningly. This is a sentiment which would undoubtedly please the major. Bennett has the makings of an officer who will do what needs to be done to achieve his aims.

'even when he was talking or rambling his face was like a clean sheet of paper, you could guess at nothing'

Although Bennett is friendly and polite, Alec finds him difficult to make out. He says that 'even when he was talking or rambling his face was like a clean sheet of paper, you could guess at nothing'. Jerry thinks he knows Bennett's type and thinks it would be a good idea to stay on Bennett's good side, as he is 'cute enough, that one, to be on the winning side in the end'.

Like Jerry, Bennett seems far older than Alec, even though they are roughly the same age. Bennett's view of the war is a cynical one. He says that the men at the front are mere 'performing dogs' and that they will attack whenever 'the fat men at home' want them to. He sees no greater glory in the war and seems uninterested in the political reasons behind it all. His initial desire for a heroic role in a battle is replaced with the realisation that he will 'probably die ignominiously of galloping foot rot'.

Bennett makes acute observations about Major Glendinning, Alec and the men in their command. He has a good understanding of human nature and says that the enlisted men will not obey Alec or Bennett but they will obey Major Glendinning because they fear him. Bennett expresses a desire to become, like the major, one of 'the whip crackers'.

Wants more of Alec than Alec can give

Bennett is, at the very least, fond of Alec. He is intrigued by the other man's view of the world and by his innocence and gentleness. One evening, as he and Alec rest in their dug-out, Alec wonders if there will be an attack soon. Bennett dismisses the notion of anything happening so soon and says, 'I love you, Alec. I love the simple way in which your mind works.' Although he is not speaking seriously, there is a hint that his feelings for Alec run a little deeper than mere friendship.

Over time, Bennett's affection for Alec seems to become stronger but Alec does not know how to respond to this. When Bennett does make his move and goes so far as to put his hand on Alec's head in a mixture of 'a benediction and a caress', Alec freezes. Bennett goes on to explain that in normal circumstances he would not make his admiration of Alec so obvious and assures Alec that he does not have to say anything in return. Alec does not react one way or the other, which disappoints Bennett. Any reaction would be better than none at all. This desire to provoke some sort of emotional response from Alec is also the reason why, the following day, Bennett takes Alec's letter from home and tears it up in front of him. None of this has the desired effect on Alec, however, and Bennett accepts this rejection graciously, moving swiftly on to other topics.

> Over time, Bennett's affection for Alec seems to become stronger but Alec does not know how to respond to this

Courteous and willing to judge people on their merits

There are elements of Bennett's character of which Major Glendinning would not approve. When Alec introduces Jerry, an enlisted man, to Bennett as their companion, Bennett responds politely and gallantly.

He holds out his hand for Jerry to shake, seemingly oblivious to Jerry's inferior social position.

Final impression

Bennett is taken to hospital while Jerry is still absent without leave, so he is not required to take a stand on one side or the other when Jerry is arrested. Therefore, we never know if Bennett would have helped Jerry or would have sided with Major Glendinning. He does seem to like Jerry and he says he does not care for rules, but at the same time he is a product of the sort of upbringing which both he and Major Glendinning say would have made Alec more like a proper officer. Perhaps he would have spoken up on Jerry's behalf or perhaps he would have stood silently by, acknowledging that in serious matters army discipline must be maintained. We will never know. Bennett is somewhat of an enigma and his abrupt departure from the novel at a crucial moment means that he is allowed to remain so.

3

The single text

Guide to the Single Text exam section

Paper 2, Ordinary Level: this section is worth **60 marks**

The Single Text is the first section examined in Paper 2. There are a number of different single texts set each year and these are listed on the first page of your exam paper along with the relevant page number.

You are only required to study **one** of these single texts.

Beware: sometimes a book you are studying as part of your Comparative Study will also appear as a Single Text option. It is vitally important that you remember that you are only to answer the Single Text questions on *How Many Miles to Babylon?* If you use your Comparative Study text in the Single Text section, you will not be able to use it in the Comparative Study section.

You are required to know your Single Text in far more detail than you know your Comparative Study texts.

Because you are studying a novel rather than a play, you do not need to learn a large number of quotes. However, if you are hoping for a high grade, it would be no harm to familiarise yourself with some of the more important quotes from the novel. A good starting point would be to learn the quotes that appear in this book.

Types of questions asked

You will be required to answer **three ten-mark questions** and **one thirty-mark question**. There is no choice in the ten-mark questions; you must answer all of them. There is a choice between three different thirty-mark questions. You need only answer one of these.

Ten-mark questions

Character

This is undoubtedly the examiners' favourite type of question. You may be asked to comment on one or more of the main characters and say why they act the way they do in the novel.

Relationships

These questions generally focus on the central relationships in the novel, all of which are covered in detail in this book.

Plot questions

In these questions, you may be asked what happens at a particular point in the novel. You must be accurate here. Do not give analysis or personal opinion when answering a question on the plot. Look at the sample answers given in this book to see how this type of question should be approached.

The world of the text/social setting

You may be asked questions about the setting of the novel and how the time and place in which they live affects the characters.

Theme or issue

You may be asked to comment on the theme of the novel.

An important moment in the text

You may be asked to describe a happy, sad, pleasant, disturbing, violent, frightening, important, amusing, enjoyable or dangerous moment. Remember, when describing this moment, to say **why** it is happy or sad etc.

The ending

You may be asked to comment on the ending. Was it what you expected? How were things resolved for various characters?

Writer's attitude towards the subject of the novel

Be sure you are able to say what this attitude is and how it is conveyed to us by her writing.

Thirty-mark questions

Many of the questions in this section are similar to the ten-mark questions. The principal difference is the length of answer expected. This type of question is effectively a short writing task, similar to the Comprehension Question B answers on Paper 1. You should bear this in mind when planning and writing your answer. The **layout** of the letter or diary entry or whatever you may be asked to do is not as important as it is in the Comprehension Question B section, but if you are looking for a high grade, you should make an effort to use appropriate language, show an awareness of your audience and generally show an understanding of how such a task should be approached.

As it is a thirty-mark question, you should be aiming to write around six paragraphs, each containing a valid point.

There is an element of personal response here, but be very careful to ensure that your answer is based on the novel. There is occasionally some scope for you to use your imagination but only in the way you express yourself. In other words, if you are asked to pretend you are one of the characters and are writing a diary entry after a significant event, you must be sure to stick to the facts of the event as they are presented in the novel. This is a test of your knowledge of the novel. Don't be fooled by seemingly vague questions or by the word 'imagine'. The answers must all be based on the Single Text itself and nothing else.

If you are asked for your opinion of the novel, try to be positive. You may not like the book but it was chosen as a good example of its genre, and you would be unwise to criticise it.

Character study

This is a very common question, as it is in the ten-mark section. In this question, you may be asked to pretend you are one of the characters in the novel, and to write the diary entry he or she might make after a significant event. Or you may be asked whether or not you could live with one of the characters. Another option may be a question requiring you to write a speech defending or prosecuting a certain character. Of course, the question may simply ask you to analyse one of the main characters, but it is more likely to be framed as a short writing task along the lines of those given in Comprehension Question B on Paper 1.

World of the text/setting

You may be asked what differences there are between the world of the text and the world in which you live. Would you like to live in the world of the text? What have you learnt about the world of the text from reading the novel? How did the setting/world of the text affect the plot and/or the characters' lives?

Relationships

These questions generally focus on the central relationships in the novel.

Review

You may be asked to write an article or a speech in which you give your opinion of the novel. In general, you will be asked to present this speech or article to an audience of your peers. In other words, you should be prepared to tell other students what you thought of the book and whether or not you would recommend it to them. Make sure to consider several different aspects of the novel when planning your answer. Is the theme one which would appeal to your peers? What about the language? Does the book move at a fast pace and keep you gripped from start to finish? Are the characters likeable? Could you relate to the issues dealt with in the novel? Did you learn anything from the novel?

Try to be as positive as you can when answering this question. Refer to the novel in every single paragraph.

Report

Here you will have to imagine that you are a reporter or possibly a police officer, writing a report on an event that has taken place in the novel.

Theme or issue

What view of life do you get from the novel? Is it uplifting or depressing? Are there life lessons to be learnt? What is the author's attitude towards the theme of the novel?

An important moment in the text

You may be asked to describe a happy, sad, pleasant, disturbing, violent, frightening, important, amusing, enjoyable or dangerous moment. Remember, when describing this moment, to say **why** it is happy or sad etc.

Alternative endings

Occasionally, you are asked to imagine how the events in the novel might have turned out if characters had made different choices. This is a difficult question to tackle as the temptation to wander far from the text itself can be great. Try to base your answer on the text in so far as it is possible to do so. Try to keep the characters' behaviour in keeping with the way they have acted throughout the novel.

Important note

The Comparative Study notes in this book are also intended to be used to help Ordinary Level students prepare for the Single Text section of the examination. For example, **themes**, the **world of the text** and **relationships** are also dealt with in the Comparative Study section and all of these are areas which should be covered by anyone studying *How Many Miles to Babylon?* as a Single Text.

Guidelines for answering exam questions

This section is worth **60 marks** and should take you a little less than an hour to complete

When you read the question, underline the key words: **describe, explain, outline,** etc.

Study the question carefully. Try to paraphrase it. What exactly are you being asked? Is the question on plot or character, for example? Is there more than one part to the question? Look for the word 'and'. This can be an indication that there are two parts to the question.

Plan your answer. It is well worth taking the time to do this.

Think in terms of key moments: this will ensure that you refer to the text and will help you to keep the sequence of events in the right order.

Do not, under any circumstances, simply summarise the plot.

Remember that, as a general rule, (although you must be guided by the question first and foremost) five marks equals one well-developed point. One well-developed point equals one paragraph. So, if a question is worth thirty marks, you should try to make at least six points. You may also wish to include a brief introduction and conclusion.

It cannot be stressed enough that, unless you are specifically asked to do so in a recall question, simply retelling the story will not get you marks. Avoid falling into the trap of simply describing the world of the text without saying what effect it has on the characters' lives.

In order to get high marks, you need to:

- *Answer the question asked (30 per cent).*
- *Make sure every paragraph develops that answer (30 per cent).*
- *Use varied and appropriate language (30 per cent).*
- *Keep an eye on your spelling and grammar (10 per cent).*

Look back over the plan. Does each point you are intending to make answer the question? Is each point backed up by an example from the text? Do the paragraphs flow logically from one to the other?

Past examination questions

Paper 2, Ordinary Level

2011   **D.** *How Many Miles to Babylon?* – Jennifer Johnston

Answer **all** of the questions.

1. (a) Describe an occasion, in the early part of the novel, which reveals the close friendship between Alec and Jerry. (10)

   (b) Do you think that the relationship between Alec and his mother was good or bad? Give one reason for your answer. (10)

2. What is your opinion of Frederick Moore, Alec's father? Explain your answer. (10)

3. Answer **one** of the following: [Each part carries 30 marks.]

(i) 'During the course of the novel Alec learns many bitter lessons: about people, social position, duty, friendship, etc.'

   Do you agree with this statement? Give reasons for your answer based on your reading of the novel.

OR

(ii) Write an article about Jennifer Johnston's *How Many Miles to Babylon?* for your school magazine in which you consider whether the novel is relevant to young people today.

OR

(iii) Imagine you are Jerry and you have been condemned to death. Write a final letter to be sent to your mother.

   You might write about your experiences in France, memories of your youth in Ireland, your friendship with Alec, your search for your father, your regrets, etc.

2008   **C.** *How Many Miles to Babylon?* – Jennifer Johnston

Answer **all** of the questions.

1. (a) Alec admits that he lacked 'team spirit'.

Do you think that he would have been a more successful person if he had been sent to school? Explain your answer. (10)

(b) Describe what happened on the last evening/night before Alec and Jerry joined the army. (10)

2. Describe a pleasant or a disturbing event in the novel and explain why you found it so. (10)

3. Answer **one** of the following: [Each part carries 30 marks.]

(i) Major Glendinning has been asked to write a report recording his opinion of Alec Moore after Alec has been executed. Write that report.

OR

(ii) '*How Many Miles to Babylon?* is a great read.'

Write an article for a magazine, in which you support or oppose the above view of the novel.

OR

(iii) Imagine that you are **either** Alec **or** Jerry. Write the letter that you would send to **either** your mother **or** father describing your war experience.

B. *How Many Miles to Babylon?* – Jennifer Johnston

2006

Answer **all** of the questions.

1. (a) Describe what life is like for Alec living at home with his mother and father. Support your views with reference to the novel. (10)

(b) '*We had great times.*'

What, in your view, are the great times Alec and Jerry had together? Explain your answer. (10)

2. Do you understand why Alec shot Jerry? Explain your answer. (10)

3. Answer **one** of the following: [Each part carries 30 marks.]

(i) Imagine that Alicia, Alec's mother, kept a diary. Write the diary entry she might have written on the day Alec went away to enlist in the army.

OR

(ii) In the beginning of the novel, Alec says – *'I love no living person.'*

From your reading of the novel, do you think that this is true? Explain your answer with reference to the text.

OR

(iii) *'It is every young man's duty to fight for his country.'*

Based on your reading of the novel, write out the speech that you would make in response to this statement.

2003

C. *How Many Miles to Babylon?* – Jennifer Johnston

Answer **all** of the questions.

1. (a) Briefly describe Alec's home life with his mother and father. (10)

(b) In your opinion, why did Alicia, Alec's mother, encourage him to go to fight in the war? (10)

2. Do you think that Alec was a good friend to Jerry? Explain your answer. (10)

3. Answer **one** of the following: [Each part carries 30 marks.]

(i) Imagine you were with Alec and Jerry on the battlefields of World War I.

Write some short diary entries telling what life was like.

OR

(ii) 'Mother, just a few lines to tell you what I think of you …'

Complete this letter from Alec to his mother, Alicia, saying the things you think he should have said to her.

OR

(iii) What is your opinion of Major Glendinning, Alec's commanding officer? Explain your opinion.

Sample answers

1. (a) Describe an occasion, in the early part of the novel, which reveals the close friendship between Alec and Jerry.

2011 10 MARKS

Comment: This question asks you to describe an occasion from the early part of the novel, so make sure you focus on something that happened before Jerry and Alec went to war.

Break your answer into as many paragraphs are necessary. Although this is only a ten-mark question, you may need to write more than two or three paragraphs in order to describe the occasion properly.

SAMPLE ANSWER 1

An occasion in the early part of the novel which I feel reveals the close friendship between Alec and Jerry is their meeting at the dance at the crossroads the night before they join the army. This meeting takes place shortly after Alicia Moore has told her son that Frederick Moore is not his father. Deeply upset by this news, Alec leaves the house and walks towards the village.

The opening sentence reflects the wording of the question

As he draws near the village, Alec comes across some villagers drinking and dancing at the crossroads. Jerry Crowe is among them. He offers Alec a drink and they fall into conversation. They discuss joining the army and, although there is a moment of tension when Alec expresses surprise that Jerry should be enlisting in the British army as he has always expressed republican sympathies, they quickly put this behind them. Jerry seems to take comfort from the fact that he and Alec will be joining up at the same time and he grips Alec's knee tightly, saying: 'We'll go together so.'

Alec tells Jerry what Alicia said about his father and Jerry points out that Alicia might have been lying, something which had never occurred to Alec. The pair drink and chat for a while more and then decide to join the dance. Alec is less used to alcohol than Jerry and falls

Words like 'loyally' show the friendship between the young men

down, drunk. The villagers laugh unkindly but Jerry loyally comes to Alec's defence. He offers to take Alec home and they head off together, arm in arm.

When they reach the lake, Jerry suggests a swim, saying that it might sober them up. As they dry off after their swim, Jerry brings up the topic of women, admitting to Alec that he has never 'been with a girl'. For all that he acts like an older man, Jerry is still young and inexperienced and it is only with Alec that he seems willing to show this side of himself.

The pair chat for a while longer until Alec complains of the cold and says it's time to go. They arrange to meet on the train the following day. Alec heads home, leaving his old friend staring at the lake and the hills, trying to fix the image forever in his mind.

The final paragraph refers back to the question and ties up the answer neatly

I believe that this meeting shows the loyalty and affection both young men feel for each other and how comfortable they feel exchanging confidences, even when they have not seen each other for some time.

10 MARKS **2011**

1. (b) Do you think that the relationship between Alec and his mother was good or bad? Give one reason for your answer.

Comment: Although most questions which offer you a choice allow you to decide for yourself which option is best, there are occasions where it would be very difficult to support one case over another. This question is one example of that. It would be almost impossible to say that Alec and his mother had a good relationship. However, if you can support your answer with quotation or reference to the novel, then you are of course free to say that the pair had a good relationship.

Note that you are asked to give one reason to back up your point of view. Key moments you may wish to discuss include the way in which Alicia tries to interfere in the relationship between Alec and Frederick Moore, her domineering behaviour, and the fact that she sends her son off to war.

SAMPLE ANSWER 2

I think that the relationship between Alec and his mother is a bad one. Alicia Moore seems to regard Alec as little more than a pawn in the deadly game she plays with her husband. She uses Alec to punish and hurt Frederick for her unhappiness in her marriage.

The nature of the relationship is defined in the opening sentence

The dreadful relationship between Alicia and Alec is clearly shown the night before Alec leaves to join the army. Alicia has been pressing him to enlist as she feels that she will bask in the reflected glory of his heroism. It is clear that she views Alec as a disappointment to her and she is bitterly resentful of the fact that – despite her best efforts – he has become like his father and is no kind of companion for her.

All the negative aspects of the relationship are highlighted in the description of this incident

Alec does not want to join the army and his refusal to do so brings out the worst side of Alicia. She reveals her true dislike of her son, claiming that he is a coward for not enlisting. Alec refuses to rise to the bait, which angers his mother. He says that he wishes to stay at home as his father needs him. Alicia seems angered by her son's fondness for his father and, in an act of almost unspeakable cruelty, she tells Alec that Frederick Moore is not his true father. Alec is appalled to hear this and asks who his real father is. Alicia downplays the importance of the whole issue, saying that Alec's biological father is dead and that she barely remembers him. She seems to care little for her son's natural upset and curiosity on hearing such news. All she wants is to break the bond between Alec and Frederick. Alec is so hurt and shocked by what his mother tells him that he decides to enlist in the army the next day.

Emotive words such as 'hurt', 'shocked', 'appalled' and 'cruelty' reinforce the negative aspects of the relationship

I believe that this incident shows how poor a relationship exists between Alicia and Alec Moore. She wants to get her own way and is prepared to hurt her son in order to do so. Not only that, but she is also keen to send him to war in order that he may become some sort of hero, and award her the status of grieving mother of a dead soldier.

The conclusion refers back to the question

2. **What is your opinion of Frederick Moore, Alec's father? Explain your answer.**

Comment: This is a question on **character**. Refer to Chapter 2 to help you prepare an answer.

SAMPLE ANSWER 3

Opinion is stated in the opening sentence

My opinion of Frederick Moore is that he is a weak but well-meaning man who is beaten down by a miserable marriage and the sense that he is a failure in life.

Frederick Moore's role in the text is mentioned

Frederick Moore serves as a foil to his wife Alicia in that he is essentially kind and undemanding, but at the same time he is not strong enough to stand up for himself or his son. Alicia is cruel, selfish and domineering and Frederick bows to her wishes because of what he describes as 'a terrible lethargy' which sets in when he knows that nothing he says or does will make any difference. We, the readers, sympathise with Frederick's position in that we see how miserable he is in his marriage, but at the same time we feel impatient at his inability to stand up to his wife when his son's life is on the line. Frederick Moore does not want Alec to go to war and he goes so far as to beg his wife not to send their only son away, but he is powerless in the face of her scorn and contempt.

I believe that, had he been married to a different woman and had he lived in a different time, Frederick Moore would most likely have been a good, if not great, father. However, married to the manipulative, bitter, disappointed Alicia and living in a time when the role of the Anglo-Irish father was to stand back and not become emotionally involved in the lives of his children, Frederick Moore is doomed to failure.

A quote is used to provide a neat conclusion

It is hard not to feel sympathy for anyone in such a position and I view Frederick Moore as almost as much a victim of circumstance as his son, Alec. I understand what Alec means when he says, on the eve of his execution, that the news of his death may kill his father but that the older man 'may be better off dead'.

3. (i) 'During the course of the novel Alec learns many bitter lessons: about people, social position, duty, friendship, etc.' Do you agree with this statement? Give reasons for your answer based on your reading of the novel.

2011 30 MARKS

Q. *What sort of task is this?*

A. This is a persuasive piece in which you are making a case.

Q. *What should the content be?*

A. The question gives you a number of prompts which you are free to use or ignore. It is generally a good idea to use at least some of the prompts, however. In this answer, the issues of social position and relationships are dealt with in some detail.

Q. *Who is my audience?*

A. There is no audience specified in this question. If this is the case, then try to imagine that you are writing for your own teacher and err on the side of caution. You will not be penalised for being too formal in your writing, but you may be penalised for using a chatty tone when it is inappropriate to do so.

Q. *What register should I use?*

A. See above.

SAMPLE ANSWER 4

Yes, I agree that Alec learns many bitter lessons about life during the course of the novel. Indeed, his view of life is so bleak by the end of the book that he faces his impending death calmly and without any apparent fear or sadness.

One of the first lessons Alec learns is that parents do not always love their children unconditionally. Alec's father is a distant, withdrawn figure who has little involvement in his young son's life. He is not unkind, but neither does he concern himself unduly with his

It is always a good idea to start at the beginning and work through the events of the book in chronological order, insofar as that is possible. If you do this, your answer will be well structured

son's well-being, choosing instead to give in to his controlling wife's demands when it comes to parenting. She is cold and aloof, and has little interest in Alec, using him as a shield between herself and the husband she despises. When Frederick Moore suggests sending Alec away to boarding school, Alicia will have none of it. This is not because she loves Alec and wants to keep him near her, it is because she does not want to be alone with her husband. Largely ignored by his parents, young Alec is more an observer than a participant in family life. He develops 'the technique of listening to a fine art', and sits quietly and miserably through many hate-filled, malevolent conversations at meal times. It is apparent to Alec that his function is simply to be a pawn in his parents' 'terrible game'. This is indeed a bitter lesson for a young child to learn.

Relevant quotes show the examiner that you have a good knowledge of the text. Remember, if you were studying a play, you would be learning a large number of quotes

His parents' unhappy marriage and his loveless childhood affects Alec in a number of ways, one of which is to make him emotionally withdrawn and generally unable to react to spontaneous overtures of liking or love. When Bennett expresses his fondness for Alec he is met with confusion and silence. Alec admits to himself that this is because 'in the life I had always known, spontaneity and warmth were unknown, almost anarchic qualities'. It is only with Jerry that Alec can truly relax and accept gestures of friendship and affection. Even then, Alec recognises that by opening himself up to friendship, he is also opening himself up to the possibility of hurt. Alec is so damaged by his dysfunctional upbringing that, by and large, he prefers to remain detached from the world rather than engage with anyone and risk being cruelly let down.

Each paragraph refers back to the question

Alec's friendship with Jerry has to be a secret because both boys know that if their families were to find out, they would put a stop to it. Alec is from a higher social class than Jerry and they live in a time and place where such things matter. When the friendship is discovered, Alec's parents unite briefly to talk to their son about the inadvisability of such a relationship. Alec's father acknowledges that it is a 'sad fact' that his son must accept 'the responsibilities and limitations of the class into which you are born'. Yet again, Alec learns that life is unfair and that he has little control over his own life. Of course, this is a message which is driven home with even greater force when he joins the army and discovers that not only is he subject to the same rules of class distinction but his very existence is in the hands of others.

One of the harshest and most depressing lessons Alec learns is that good does not necessarily triumph over evil. His mother is a self-absorbed, cruel woman, but it is she who calls the shots in the family home. Frederick Moore is a kindly, if somewhat weak, man but he is reduced to utter misery and loneliness by his wife's implacable hatred and contempt. When Alec enlists, he finds himself thrown into a world where there seems to be no justice and where might is right. Jerry is sentenced to death for obeying his mother's wishes and going to look for his missing father. Nothing Alec says or does can change the fact that Jerry will die, but still he pleads with Major Glendinning. When this fails to achieve the desired effect, Alec asks the major where he learned to be so evil. The major is unmoved and simply replies, 'The world taught me. It will teach you.' To Alec's credit, he never learns this lesson but instead remains true to himself and his own values: loyalty, selflessness and kindness.

It is admirable that, even in the face of such depressing and negative messages about love and life, Alec does not waver in his affection and loyalty towards his childhood friend. That he should be sentenced to death for doing so is merely a final affirmation that there is nothing worth living for.

1. (a) Alec admits that he lacked 'team spirit'.
    Do you think that he would have been a more successful person if he had been sent to school? Explain your answer.

2008 | 10 MARKS

Comment: Look at the question carefully and examine all the parts of it. Before you begin your answer, think about Alec's character for a moment. Do you agree that he lacked 'team spirit'? Or did he just lack the kind of team spirit that people like Major Glendinning and his mother wanted him to display? Did he get on well with anyone? Was he unsuccessful in all his relationships? Did going to school help his father to be more successful than his son?

Once you have decided on your approach, make a very brief plan.

SAMPLE ANSWER 5

Opening lines reflect the wording of the question

No, I do not think Alec would have been a more successful person if he had been sent to school. In fact, I think he is a successful person but is not viewed as such by those around him simply because he is unwilling and unable to live up to their expectations. I also believe that Alec's nature is such that he is not easily influenced by others and would, therefore, have grown into the sort of man he became regardless of his educational background.

Two main points are briefly introduced

First point – that Alec is a successful person – is developed

The sort of 'team spirit' that Major Glendinning wants Alec to have is not a very admirable one. The fact that Alec is friendly with Jerry angers the major, who feels that officers should not fraternise with enlisted men. In the major's book, 'team spirit' means being part of the right team and playing by the rules, regardless of how discriminatory and harsh such rules may be. I believe that Alec's friendship with Jerry does show team spirit in the truest sense of the words. It takes courage and loyalty on Alec's part to remain loyal to his childhood companion in the face of such strong disapproval and opposition.

Second point – that Alec is quite stubborn in some ways and unlikely to cave in to pressure to change – is developed

If Alec had gone to school, I doubt that the authorities or his fellow pupils would have been able to change his personality very much. He seems quietly stubborn in his own way and ignores the pressures of those who attempt to make him behave according to their rules. After all, his parents try to talk the young Alec out of his affection for Jerry but they do not succeed in doing so. Alec may appear weak, but he has a core of strength underneath his quiet, mild-mannered exterior. His actions at the end of the book, when he shoots Jerry, show that Alec is willing to face anything, even his own death, rather than allow his friend to face the firing squad. I cannot imagine that going to school would have made a significant difference to someone who is capable of such an act of courage and selflessness.

SAMPLE ANSWER 6

Yes, I think that if Alec had gone to school he would have become a more successful person. He says himself that as a youngster he was 'isolated from the surrounding children of my own age'. Because he is a lonely little boy, young Alec quickly becomes very attached to Jerry Crowe and comes to value their friendship more than anything else in the world. Had he gone to school, he would have had the opportunity to befriend lots of other boys and would have had a greater sense of perspective when it came to relationships. This friendship with Jerry ultimately proves his undoing as he is unable to cope with the thought of life without his only true friend. Instead he takes the decision to spare Jerry death by firing squad by shooting him and thus ensures that he, Alec, would be executed. Alec admits at the start of the book that he doesn't love any 'living person'. I think that if he had gone to school, he would have had more friends and that might have given him a reason to live.

I think that going to school would also have given Alec the chance to partially escape the unhealthy influence of his mother. Her manipulative, unloving attitude towards him seems to have given him a negative view of women and of relationships in general. He reacts to her coldness by withdrawing into himself and cutting himself off from very close ties with others, apart from Jerry. When Bennett tries to provoke emotional reactions in Alec, he fails because, as Alec admits, he is 'unable to react' to 'spontaneity and warmth'. Had he gone to school, he would more than likely have spent time in other boys' houses and seen parents quite unlike his own: parents who loved one another and their children. This might have enabled Alec to be more successful in his relationships with others later in life. As it is, the only person with whom he is able to be affectionate is Jerry, and the loss of Jerry leaves him bereft.

Opening line reflects the wording of the question

In this answer, the two points being made are not introduced in a brief introduction. Either approach is acceptable for a ten-mark question at Ordinary Level

Points are supported with suitable quotation and reference

10 2008
MARKS

1. (b) Describe what happened on the last evening/night before Alec and Jerry joined the army.

Comment: This type of question requires you to have good recall of the events of the novel. You would be expected to include their drinking, dancing, swimming in the lake and you should also mention some of the things Jerry and Alec discuss.

Even though this is only a ten-mark question, it is worth taking a moment or two to write a brief plan. This will ensure that you write the events in chronological order.

SAMPLE ANSWER 7

Events are given in chronological order

This is a recall question, so there is no need for any analysis of the events

The same level of detail is given throughout the answer

The night before Alec and Jerry leave to join the army, Alec goes for a walk. He hears music and follows the sound. When he draws near to the village Alec finds that a group of local people are drinking and dancing at the crossroads. Jerry is there and he offers Alec a drink. Jerry tells Alec that he is enlisting in the army the following day. Alec is surprised that his old friend is joining the British army and says that he thought Jerry was 'with the Shinners'. Jerry angrily tells Alec to shut up, but quickly recovers himself, saying that he is a little drunk and insisting that it is only cash that is making him join up. However, he admits later on that he is also hoping that his military training will help him in the fight for Irish independence. Alec tells Jerry that he too is planning to join up the following day. He also tells Jerry about his mother's claim that he is not his father's son.

As the night wears on, Alec becomes very drunk and dances until he falls down. The villagers laugh mockingly but Jerry helps his friend to his feet and they half walk, half crawl along the path towards Alec's home. In an effort to sober up, they go for a swim in the lake. It is almost morning when they get out of the water.

Before going their separate ways, the two young men look at the countryside around them and try to fix the image in their minds so that they can remember it when they are far from home. They shake hands and say that they will meet again at the train station. Alec walks home, leaving Jerry standing by the lake, staring at the hills.

2. Describe a pleasant or a disturbing event in the novel and explain why you found it so.

2008 **10** MARKS

Comment: Note the word 'and' in this question. You have to do two things in your answer: describe the event and explain why you chose it as an example of a pleasant or disturbing event.

You could write a paragraph describing the event and then write a second paragraph explaining why you found it pleasant or disturbing, or you could comment on the event as you describe it.

A brief introduction and conclusion outlining your views help to keep the answer focused.

SAMPLE ANSWER 8

I believe that the conversation between Alec and his mother the night before Alec leaves home to enlist in the army is a particularly disturbing moment in the novel. The reason I find it so disturbing is that it is a perversion of what I would expect of a conversation between a mother and a son on the eve of the son's departure for war.

The opening paragraph immediately addresses the question

The conversation takes place in Alec's room after dinner. Alicia asks him again to join the army, saying that it means a lot to her. When he refuses, she calls him a coward. Alec does not rise to this bait, and repeats his refusal. He points out that his father needs him. His mother seems angered by his fondness for his father and she selfishly points out that she sacrificed any chance of happiness by staying with her husband for Alec's sake. All she asks for in return, she says, is that her son should join the army. It is obvious that she wants the glory that comes with being the mother of a hero. Again, Alec refuses to go. I find it extremely disturbing that a mother would want her son to fight in the war so that she could bask in his reflected glory and so that she could

A detailed description of the moment is given, followed by an explanation as to why it is particularly disturbing

deprive her husband of his son.

Again, the reason for the disturbing nature of the moment is highlighted

When she realises that Alec wants to stay to help his father, Alicia Moore plays her trump card. Cruelly, she tells Alec that Frederick Moore is not his father, although the old man does not know it. Alec is horrified and asks who his real father is. His mother says that he is dead and that she barely remembers him anyway. It seems that she will stop at nothing to make Alec join the army. She admits that she is 'not a nice woman' but claims that it is partly her unhappy life that has made her this way. She leaves, saying as she does so that her wish for Alec to join the army is motivated by 'all the right reasons as well as a few of the wrong ones'. I cannot believe this. It seems to me that Alec's mother is an evil woman who will do whatever it takes to get her own way.

The concluding paragraph sums up the reason for finding this moment disturbing

It is this twisted relationship between a mother and her son that leaves me deeply disturbed. Certainly, there are descriptions of far more gruesome events later in the book, but that is when Alec is at the front line. Major Glendinning may send men into battle knowing they are likely to be killed, and the Germans may shoot at the British soldiers, but that is the nature of war. For a mother to want her son to risk his life in those circumstances for her own selfish ends is, I believe, far more chilling than anything else that happens in the novel.

30 MARKS **2008**

3. (iii) Imagine that you are **either** Alec **or** Jerry. Write the letter that you would send to **either** your mother **or** father describing your war experience.

Q. *What sort of task is this?*
A. This is an informal letter.

Q. *What should the content be?*
A. You must describe your war experience. You could talk about the fear, the discomfort and the illnesses that are part of life in the trenches. Or you could, as is the case in this letter, try to play down the

worst aspects of your war experience in order to stop your elderly father from worrying too much. You could also refer to the letter Frederick Moore sent Alec shortly after Christmas.

Q. *Who is my audience?*

A. In this case, Alec is speaking to his father. Although they do feel affectionate towards one another, they never express their feelings openly, so it would be inappropriate to do so in this letter.

Q. *What register should I use?*

A. You should try to reflect the formal way in which Alec and his father speak to one another during the novel. You should also bear in mind that Alec is well educated, so would be likely to use a rich and varied vocabulary. Slang or an overly-chatty tone would be inappropriate here.

SAMPLE ANSWER 9 –

A LETTER FROM ALEC TO HIS FATHER

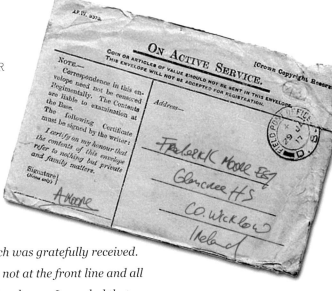

West Outre,

Flanders,

Belgium.

1st January, 1915

Dear Father,

Thank you for your recent letter, which was gratefully received. Time passes slowly here when we are not at the front line and all communications from home are most welcome. I am glad that you are enjoying the hunting this season and that Morrigan is coming along so well.

We are stationed in a farmhouse some distance from the front at the moment, catching up on some rest and recuperation. I think you would be surprised by how routine and dull our lives are here most of the time. I'm sure that news of the recent heavy losses at Ypres have caused you concern but there is little need to worry. We have seen virtually no action to date and I have not fired my pistol or rifle once. Yes, there is shellfire when we are at the front and there is always the danger of enemy snipers picking off an unwary soldier who pops his head above the parapet, but as you know, I am not the sort to seek out danger in any form. Even when I am at the front, I spend much of my time in the officers' dug-out, reading and writing. When I patrol the trenches, I make sure to keep my head well down at all times. I hope this reassures you somewhat and that you can look forward to my safe return with more certainty.

You are no doubt wondering what sort of life we are living here. Our daily routine depends on where we are stationed. When we are at the front, it's a question of shoring up the defences and raising the duckboards above the level of the water. If this is not done regularly, the enlisted men are soon standing in several feet of water. It's quite tedious work, but my job is mainly to supervise the repairs rather than actually do the physical labour myself. Still, sometimes it's a question of all hands on deck when there has been heavy shelling and the trench is in a bad way. We only spend a few days at the front before moving back to the safer reserve trenches for several more days. Every two weeks or so we come back to this farmhouse for a rest. When I first came here, I thought a derelict farmhouse was a poor place to spend a few days, but it seems like a positive paradise after the mud and cold of the trenches.

Before I left home, you asked me to tell you if there was anything I needed, and I have been giving the matter some thought. If it would not be too much trouble, I would appreciate several pairs of thick woollen socks. There are very few opportunities to wash our clothes or ourselves here and the damp of the trenches combined with the regular marches means that our feet and socks are soon in a dreadful state. I have heard it said that an army marches on its stomach, but I must say that in my experience an army marches very firmly on its blistered, chilblain-covered, evil-smelling feet. I would happily forego a meal for a pair of dry socks and some more chilblain ointment.

Moving on to more pleasant matters, I think you will be pleased to hear that, even in this rather godforsaken place, we have managed to find horses to ride and Lieutenant Bennett and I have enjoyed some good gallops through the local countryside. Still, it is no substitute for the woods and fields of Wicklow and I look forward to taking up my hunt duties again as soon as this mess is over. Keep Morrigan in trim for me and tell Charlie Brennan not to get too comfortable in my huntsman's coat as I'll be home before long. Bennett tells me that the news from England is that we are winning the war. The sooner the better, I say.

I remain your loving son,
Alec

3. (iii) Imagine that you are **either** Alec **or** Jerry. Write the letter that you would send to **either** your mother **or** father describing your war experience.

2008 **30** MARKS

Q. *What sort of task is this?*
A. This is an informal letter.

Q. *What should the content be?*
A. You must describe your war experience. You could talk about the fear, the discomfort and the illnesses that are part of life in the trenches.

Q. *Who is my audience?*
A. In this case, Jerry is speaking to his mother.

Q. *What register should I use?*
A. Jerry would be unlikely to use very formal language or to possess a rich vocabulary. His sentences would be shorter than Alec's as Jerry is less well-educated than Alec and therefore less likely to have an excellent grasp of grammar. Some slang or colloquialisms would be appropriate here.

SAMPLE ANSWER 10 – A LETTER FROM JERRY TO HIS MOTHER

West Outre,

Flanders,

Belgium.

1st January, 1915

Dear Mother,

Thank you and the girls for the Christmas card you sent me. I should have written to you before now but we've been kept busy since we arrived, and even when I did have some free time, I didn't have any writing paper. I got some today from Alec Moore. You remember him, I'm sure. He's one of the Moores from the Big House. He's an officer now but we still talk every so often. He's a decent man.

Life here is nothing like Da said it would be. The days are long and boring at best, and terrifying at worst. I am in fear of my life and never know when a shell or bullet might end it all for me.

We have settled into a sort of a routine now, but it's not one I think I'll ever get used to. It's three days at the front, three days in the reserve trenches, then three days at the front again. Every few weeks we march back to this old farm and have five or six days off before the whole thing starts all over again.

The days at the front are the worst. The trenches are no better than deep ditches in the muddy ground and we have to share them with the living and the dead. Last week O'Keefe and myself were sent to repair a collapsed section and when we moved some of the fallen boards and sandbags, we uncovered the rotting bodies of three French soldiers. There is no time to bury men properly here, so we put them in a shallow grave and covered them as best we could. I hope that someone will do the same for me if I meet the same fate as those poor lads.

You might think that dead bodies are the worst things we could be

sharing the trenches with, but the living creatures give us far more trouble. We are all crawling with lice and fleas and we are plagued with rats. They have grown huge and brave with so much flesh to feed on. I don't suppose I'll make much of a meal for them when my number's up. I'm skinnier than I was when I left home, and that's saying something. I'd give anything to sit down to a proper meal. You never appreciate what you've got until it's too late.

It's not bad all the time, though. When we're at the farmhouse for a few days, we can sometimes have a bit of craic. Alec Moore's officer friend managed to get hold of a few horses one day and we went for a bit of a gallop. It was nice to be doing something normal for a change, and the other officer wasn't a bad fellow, for an Englishman. The horses weren't up to much, though. I felt sorry for the creatures. They had been fine beasts once but they were in very bad condition by the time we got hold of them. I wish I could transfer to the horse lines to help out but the major won't hear of it. I tell you, I couldn't hate the Germans more than I hate that major. The feeling's mutual, though. He has no time for the Irish at all and doesn't trouble himself to hide his disgust when he speaks to us. I wouldn't care what he thought if he didn't have the power to make our lives even more miserable than they are already. We're supposed to be resting while we're here, but I hear Sergeant Barry shouting at the men in the other barn, telling them that it's time for some drilling. He'll be over here in a minute to drag the rest of us out too. I'd better sign off, I suppose.

Give my love to my sisters and tell them I'll write again when I get the chance. I hope that things are a bit easier at home now that you have money from me and Da. It's hard earned, I can tell you that much.

Your loving son,
Jerry

10 2006
MARKS

1. (a) Describe what life is like for Alec living at home
        with his mother and father.
        Support your views with reference to the novel.

SAMPLE ANSWER 11

Short but relevant quotes from the novel support the points being made

In the early part of the novel, Alec states simply that 'as a child I was alone'. He is the only child of distant, withdrawn parents who show him little affection and whose hatred for one another makes Alec's home life tense and unhappy. Furthermore, Alec is isolated from the local children because he is from a wealthy Anglo-Irish family and is not permitted to mix socially with people from a lower social class. When Alicia Moore discovers that Alec has befriended Jerry Crowe, she does her level best to put a stop to the relationship, while at the same time offering no alternative source of friendship for her lonely son. Frederick Moore supports her in this, telling Alec that it is 'a sad fact' that he must accept the 'responsibilities and limitations' of his social class.

It is important to explain the effect these incidents had on Alec's home life. Each paragraph or point must link back to the question

Were Alec to be permitted to go to boarding school like most boys of his age and social background, he might have had some hope of making new friends. However, his mother will not hear of his being sent away as she despises her husband and refuses to be alone with him. Alec is forced to stay at home with his bitter, disappointed parents and endure the silences or the tense, unhappy conversations. He is little more than a pawn in the 'terrible game' his parents play with one another.

Frederick Moore is essentially a kindly man and wants to do what is right for his son, but he is too weak to stand up to his wife. He recognises that his son is lonely so, when Alec is old enough, Frederick tries to help him by involving him in estate business. Alec and his father begin to spend more time together but Alicia soon puts a stop to this potential source of happiness. Jealous and angry that Alec prefers to be with his father than with her, she determines to send her son off to war. When Alec protests, saying that he wants to stay at home to help his father, Alicia cruelly tells him that Frederick is not his real father, thereby severing any ties Alec might have had with his home and family.

Given his sad and lonely upbringing, it is little wonder that Alec has no desire to contact his parents when he is sentenced to death and only has a short time left to live.

2. Do you understand why Alec shot Jerry? Explain your answer.

SAMPLE ANSWER 12

I believe Alec shoots Jerry in an act of love, loyalty and selflessness. He knows that there is no hope whatsoever for Jerry and so he decides to take matters into his own hands and give his friend as swift and merciful a death as possible.

You are free to give your own interpretation of Alec's actions but it is important to support your viewpoint with accurate reference to the text

Jerry's fate is sealed the moment he returns to the farmhouse and seeks out his old friend. He has little option but to return and face his punishment because, as he puts it himself, there is 'no hole to hide in round here that I wouldn't be blown out of by one side or the other'.

Alec does his best to speak up for Jerry but it is no use. Jerry is sentenced to death and Alec is given the job of commanding the firing squad. In a clumsy effort at a sort of kindness, Major Glendinning advises Alec to ensure that his men shoot straight so that Jerry will be killed as quickly and cleanly as possible. I think that this advice is partly responsible for Alec's decision to give his friend a quick death by shooting him himself rather than risking the possibility of Jerry meeting a slow and painful end.

Several reasons are given for Alec's decision to shoot Jerry

By shooting Jerry, Alec not only spares him the horror of facing a firing squad but he also spares him an agonising wait in his prison cell. Jerry tells Alec that 'each hour seems so long' and says that he has not been allowed to keep any possessions that he might use to take his own life.

Alec knows that shooting Jerry will inevitably lead to his own death by firing squad but he loves his friend so dearly that he is willing to face this rather than allow Jerry to suffer any more than is absolutely necessary. The prospect of death itself does not worry Alec because, without Jerry, life will not be worth living.

30 **2006**
MARKS

3. (i) Imagine that Alicia, Alec's mother, kept a diary. Write the diary entry she might have written on the day Alec went away to enlist in the army.

Q. *What sort of task is this?*
A. This is a diary entry.

Q. *What should the content be?*
A. Diary entries reflect the writer's private thoughts and feelings. In your answer you should try to refer to events in the text. It can be tempting to go off the point but remember that this is a test of your knowledge of and reaction to the set text.

Q. *Who is my audience?*
A. Alicia is talking to herself, so she will probably be honest and quite outspoken.

Q. *What register should I use?*
A. You should try to reflect the formal way in which Alicia speaks during the novel. You should also bear in mind that Alicia is well educated, so would be likely to use a rich and varied vocabulary. Slang or an overly chatty tone would be inappropriate here.

SAMPLE ANSWER 13

What a day! I am quite exhausted from it all and feel that I made the right decision by retiring to my bedroom rather earlier than usual. Not that there was much point in remaining downstairs with Frederick. He is never good company but he seems to have given himself up to complete despair since Alexander left this morning. Typically selfish of him. He might consider my feelings. After all, I'm the boy's mother and, as such, far more deserving of sympathy than his father.

I must admit that I was disappointed by the hastiness of Alexander's departure. I had hoped that he and I could visit the Boyles later this week. It would have been most gratifying to see their admiration for Alexander's bravery in enlisting. They will be dreadfully worried about me, I imagine, now that they have lost Christopher and know the sacrifice I have made by allowing my only son to join up.

Still, there may be something to be salvaged from Alexander's ridiculous, melodramatic behaviour. It will cause quite a stir when people hear he has gone. I think I will let it be known, discreetly of course, that this has been planned for some time but that Frederick and I did not wish to make a fuss about what was, after all, the right and natural impulse of a brave young man. He is only doing his duty, I shall say. Nothing to boast about. Yes. That will do nicely. I am not as cross with Alexander as I have a right to be. After all, he has done what I asked, even if the manner of his going was not according to my plan.

I think perhaps Alexander was rather more shocked than I had expected by the news that Frederick is not his father. He became quite tiresome when I told him, claiming that he was 'dispossessed in a sentence'. I really don't see why he had to carry on so. It's not as if Frederick is such an admirable man that anyone would be proud to have him as a father. Quite the opposite, I would have thought. Still, on reflection, I think I made the right decision. If I hadn't told the boy, he would be here still, becoming ever more involved with Frederick's dreary life. My dear! Hunts, fields, tillage, cattle … it's all too tedious for words. Alexander is far better where he is.

This is a test of your knowledge of Alicia's character, so the piece should be consistent with what we know of her motives and behaviour

Alicia is very selfish and the writing reflects that. She sees all the events in terms of how they affect her

Close reference to the text and even quotation – if possible – shows a good knowledge of the novel

The tone of the piece is quite formal, even though it is a diary entry. This is appropriate, considering the time in which the novel is set, and the social class to which Alicia belongs

I do hope that there is time for Alexander to visit before he is sent to the front. Is there any way, I wonder, to find out when he might be expected to come and see us? If I knew that, I could arrange a little luncheon party or perhaps afternoon tea for some of our neighbours. How splendid it would be to have my son, the dashing young officer, arrive into the middle of such a gathering. He is a good looking boy and the uniform should suit him quite well.

I wonder where Alexander will be sent? Christopher Boyle died in Flanders; I forget exactly where. Some place with an unpronounceable name, irritatingly. It would sound quite romantic to have one's son die in a place with a beautiful French name, if one's son has to die, of course. Heaven forbid. Nobody would wish for such a thing but facts must be faced. Men do die in war and mothers must prepare themselves to greet such news with courage and dignity. Evelyn Boyle would have been well-advised to have planned a more fitting reaction than the rather noisy and inelegant weeping she fell into on receiving the telegram from the War Office. And (I can only say this to you, dear diary) black is not her colour. She will look simply terrible in mourning. I am fortunate in that black rather suits me. If the worst should happen, I will present a good front in my mourning clothes.

Goodness. All this reflection has made me lose track of time. I shall ring for the maid and go straight to bed. The events of the day have quite worn me out.

2003

1. (a) Briefly describe Alec's home life with his mother and father.

Comment: Although less detail is required in this case, this question is very similar to one that was asked in 2006. Refer to the sample answer for that year on page 112.

1. (b) In your opinion, why did Alicia, Alec's mother, encourage
    him to go to fight in the war?

2003 | 10 MARKS

Comment: This is a test of your knowledge of the text and of Alicia Moore's character. You are free to choose any reasons for Alicia sending Alec to fight in the war, as long as you can support them with suitable quotations or references. There is no right or wrong answer here. However, it is undoubtedly easier to say that Alicia's reasons are selfish and cruel than it is to say that she has good reasons for encouraging her only son to enlist. There is little in the novel to support any view other than that Alicia is a villain.

SAMPLE ANSWER 14

I think Alicia's motives for encouraging Alec to go and fight in the war are entirely selfish. She claims that she wants him to go for 'all the right reasons as well as a few of the wrong ones', but I do not believe her. Nothing in her behaviour up to this point in the novel makes me think that she does anything for any reason other than to please herself.

This answer requires you to argue a case, so your language can be quite forceful

Alicia's original plans for Alec were that he would become an interesting companion for her and would become the man her husband was not. However, she is disappointed in this and is frustrated to discover that Alec is more excited about the horse Frederick has bought him than he is about the four months spent touring Europe with her. I feel sure that Alicia decides to send Alec away in order to hurt Frederick and to get some vicarious glory for herself as the mother of a serving officer.

Evidence from the text supports the points being made

I believe that Alicia Moore supports the war effort simply because her husband does not. When he reads of John Redmond's call to Irishmen to enlist, Frederick Moore is disgusted. Alicia immediately supports Redmond, saying that he is 'behaving at last in a responsible fashion'. The timing of Alicia's announcement that Alec will be leaving for the war further convinces me that she has no 'right reasons' for

Close reference and quotations are appropriate in Single Text answers

virtually forcing her son to enlist. It appears to be Christopher Boyle's death and the attention such news attracts which prompts Alicia to decide, seemingly on the spur of the moment, that Alec must join up.

Alec has no desire to become a soldier and wishes only to stay at home and help his father run the estate. When he tells Alicia as much, she plays her trump card. She cruelly tells Alec that Frederick is not his father, thereby removing his reason for staying. This shows how little Alicia cares for her son's feelings and how determined she is to send him off to fight.

The conclusion summarises the main points

When Alec leaves the following morning, Alicia is not at all upset. Indeed, she seems positively triumphant, which indicates that she derives personal pleasure from his joining up. I believe that Alicia is delighted to have killed two birds with one stone. She has deeply hurt the husband she despises and has turned her disappointing son into a potential hero. These cruel and selfish motives are the reasons Alicia is so keen to send her only son to war.

30 MARKS **2003**

3. (ii) 'Mother, just a few lines to tell you what I think of you …'
Complete this letter from Alec to his mother, Alicia, saying the things you think he should have said to her.

Q. *What sort of task is this?*
A. This is an informal letter.

Q. *What should the content be?*
A. This task requires you to analyse Alec's feelings towards his mother and reflect them in the form of a rather outspoken letter. It would be appropriate to refer to specific incidents in the novel which showed the dysfunctional relationship between mother and son.

Q. *Who is my audience?*
A. In this case, Alec is speaking to his mother. As he knows he will never see her again, he is likely to be quite reckless and open in what he says.

Q. *What register should I use?*

A. You should try to reflect the formal way in which Alicia and Alec's father speak to one another during the novel. You should also bear in mind that Alec is well educated, so would be likely to use a rich and varied vocabulary. Slang or an overly chatty tone would be inappropriate here.

SAMPLE ANSWER 15

Flanders,
Belgium.

20th February, 1915

Mother,

Just a few lines to tell you what I think of you. I have neither the time nor the inclination to write you a lengthy letter but circumstances here have altered rather considerably in the last few days and this is likely to be my last chance to speak to you honestly. You will find out in due course why this is the case. Indeed, you may already have received some news which will make my meaning clear. If not, then you will learn soon enough. For now, it is sufficient to say that there is no reason any longer for me to maintain any pretence that you or I care about each other or that I should show you the respect due a loving mother.

You are not, and never have been, a loving mother. Recent events have made it clearer than ever to me that I grew up without love and that I am utterly alone in the world. Your only interest in me was as a substitute companion and as a pawn in the terrible game you played with my father. He is my father, by the way, whatever you may say. I am more convinced than ever that you told me that story in order to ensure that I enlisted. It was a monstrously cruel thing to do, but quite in keeping with your character. I do not believe you would stop at anything to get your own way, even if that means destroying the lives

The question does not specify when Alec should write this letter but it is possible that he might be moved to speak honestly to his mother when he knows he will never see her again

References to events in the novel support the points being made

of your own husband and son.

Once I realised the extent of your utter selfishness and your ruthlessness, I understood more about my miserable childhood. You never once considered my well-being, my feelings or my wishes. Do you remember, for example, when you decided that I should learn the piano? You arranged lessons with that unfortunate tutor from Dublin but you dismissed him suddenly on the basis of his poverty and lack of social graces. You didn't care that he needed the money or that perhaps I needed a tutor. You said you'd teach me yourself but you soon gave up. It was obvious to me that you were bored and impatient at what I came to see as my clumsy, childish fumbling at the keys.

I was terribly lonely as a child. Do you care? I doubt it. You didn't care then. When Father suggested I go away to school, you soon put a stop to that idea. Perhaps I would have made friends there. Perhaps not. I did manage to make one friend, despite your best efforts. 'That boy', you call him. Jerry Crowe. I was happy with Jerry, so I suppose I should not have been surprised when you did your best to end our friendship. Your snobbery could not allow you even to contemplate my having a friend from the village, could it?

Perhaps I can understand a little of your reasoning in not wishing me to be friends with Jerry. I don't agree with you, but I do accept that you are not alone among our social class in disapproving of such friendships. What I cannot understand, however, is why you were not content to see Father and me becoming closer in recent times. It afforded us both some measure of happiness but you destroyed even that by telling me that he is not my real father and by sending me off to war. I cannot forgive you for hurting me and Father so deeply.

You hoped that I would become a brave hero, didn't you? I never became the companion you wanted, so you decided to sacrifice me instead. You probably thought you couldn't lose. If I returned, you would be the mother of a victorious officer, and if I were killed, you would revel in the role of heartbroken mother. It gives me some small measure of satisfaction to know that I have denied you either pleasure. You will understand what I mean by that soon enough.

At the start of the novel, Alec says that he will not tell his parents about his impending execution but will allow the War Office to do so instead

I see that this short note has, despite my original intentions, become quite a long letter. I wonder if you will rip open the bulky envelope eagerly, hoping I have written something you can share with your friends? Well, I have denied you that pleasure too. I can't imagine you will want anyone to know what I think of you. I cannot know if these words will touch you or move you at all, but I feel better for having written them. Goodbye, Mother.

Alec

3. (iii) What is your opinion of Major Glendinning, Alec's commanding officer?
   Explain your opinion.

2003 **30** MARKS

Comment: This is a question on character. Refer to Chapter 2 to help you prepare an answer.

Q. *What sort of task is this?*
A. This is a persuasive piece. You are giving your opinion of Major Glendinning.

Q. *What should the content be?*
A. You should use key moments in the text to support the points you make about Major Glendinning. A quick revision of the notes on Major Glendinning's character (Chapter 2) should help you plan this answer.

Q. *Who is my audience?*
A. There is no audience specified in this question. If this is the case, then try to imagine that you are writing for your own teacher and err on the side of caution. You will not be penalised for being too formal in your writing but you may be penalised for using a chatty tone when it is inappropriate to do so.

Q. *What register should I use?*
A. See above.

SAMPLE ANSWER 16

I believe that Major Glendinning is a complex character who has traces of compassion and kindness hidden beneath a hard, well controlled exterior.

It is a good idea to trace the development of a character throughout the course of the novel. This helps to keep your answer structured

My first impression of the major is almost overwhelmingly negative. He seems to be a tough, unsympathetic man who despises the lack of professional soldiering spirit in the Irish men he has been assigned. He views the men in his charge as part of the war machine and says he will 'give no quarter' if anyone disobeys him. In many ways, the major is a mirror image of Alicia Moore. Like her, he disapproves of Alec's friendship with Jerry and does his best to mould Alec into the sort of soldier he wants. He fails in this and is disgusted by Alec's continued loyalty towards his childhood friend.

Make sure that each point about the major's character is supported by a key moment in the text

Major Glendinning is not without compassion, though he hides it well. He may treat the men as if they were part of a machine, but he does know that they have lives and worries of their own. When Alec requests compassionate leave for Jerry, the major refuses but asks Alec if he has thought about 'how many men in the British Expeditionary Force have fathers, brothers, sons, cousins missing, wounded, dead'. The fact that he even asks Alec the question shows that the major has given some thought to the suffering and loss of the men in his charge.

An incident which shows all the facets of Major Glendinning's character occurs when he goes out into No Man's Land to see to the wounded soldier who has been lying there, screaming in agony, for four days. Major Glendinning acts quickly and decisively. He bravely goes out to the injured man and, when he sees that there is nothing that can be done for him, he quickly and efficiently kills him. His manner is brisk and matter-of-fact when he embarks on what he calls 'an outing', but the major does display some emotion. He swears aloud when he sees the extent of the soldier's injuries and sighs 'a long sad sigh' as he ends the soldier's life and the screaming stops.

Although he may feel pity and sorrow, the major does his utmost to keep his feelings in check. He tries his best to teach Alec to behave in the same way, assuring him that he will be better off when he too can view the men as little more than cattle. Alec's stubborn refusal to act unemotionally threatens the major's own ability to keep his feelings in check. This can be seen in the final pages of the novel when Jerry is arrested for going absent without leave. Once again, the major tries to impress upon Alec the necessity of putting his loyalty to the army above his loyalty to his friend. When Alec calls the British army uniform 'some sort of fancy dress', Major Glendinning reacts emotionally. He pales, strikes Alec across the face with his cane and sits down again, hands trembling. It is clear that Alec has the ability to get under the major's skin and cause him to lose his self-control.

For all that he is disgusted with Alec's behaviour and determined to see Jerry's execution carried out correctly, the major does make one last effort to get through to Alec. He tries to explain to him that Jerry's death is necessary and that the best thing Alec can do is ensure that his men fire straight and give Jerry a relatively quick death. In his own way, Major Glendinning seems to regard this advice as kindly, and he seems pleased at Alec's silent nod in response. He appears to think that he has at last brought Alec around to his way of thinking. He has not, and we never learn of his reaction to Alec's final act of disobedience.

My final impression of Major Glendinning is that he is a determined, professional soldier who has devoted himself wholeheartedly to the war effort and has decided that the best way to achieve success is not to question orders but to follow such orders to the letter. Naturally, he wants his junior officers and his men to have the same attitude and he cannot and does not tolerate any deviation from this chain of command. He may have traces of compassion but he works hard to suppress any feelings which may lead him to have sympathy to his men and see them as individuals rather than as part of the war machine.

4

The comparative study

How Many Miles to Babylon?

In this chapter you will find comprehensive notes on using *How Many Miles to Babylon?* as a text for your Comparative Study. Each of the comparative modes for Higher Level and Ordinary Level is covered. As the modes change each year, it is important to check which modes apply to the year you will be sitting your Leaving Certificate.

Some of the modes for Higher and Ordinary Level overlap. Where this is the case, one set of notes is given for the two modes.

It is very important to be able to compare the texts you are studying but you should also bear in mind that at both Higher and Ordinary  Level you will usually have the option of answering a thirty-mark question on one of the texts. Students wishing to see how this text can be compared to a number of other texts on the Leaving Certificate course should refer to Naomi Kloss's comprehensive guide: *The Comparative Study: A Structured Approach*, published by Educate.ie.

These notes are designed as a reference guide to help students to put together their own Comparative Study essays. In some cases, headings and bullet points are used for clarity and to make revision easier, but students should not use either in their answers.

There is a certain amount of overlap between the comparative modes, particularly in terms of key moments, but this is inevitable. A key moment can show aspects of the central relationship, the literary genre and the cultural context, for example. As you will only be answering on one mode in the examination, this overlap is not a problem.

In this book, key moments are woven into the Comparative Study notes. As a key moment is described, its relevance to the mode is discussed and explored in detail. Remember, you should never discuss an event in your chosen text without linking it to the point you are making.

Important note

The Comparative Study notes in this book are also intended to be used to help Ordinary Level students prepare for the Single Text section of the examination. For example, **themes**, **the world of the text** (cultural context/social setting) and **relationships** are dealt with in the Comparative Study section, and all of these are areas which should be covered by anyone studying *How Many Miles to Babylon?* as a Single Text.

Literary Genre

Higher Level

Past questions on this mode of comparison have tended to focus on the following:

- *How memorable characters are created in the text*
- *How emotional power is created in the text*
- *Aspects of narrative and how they contribute to your response to the text*
- *How powerful moments add to the story in the text*
- *How the unexpected contributes to the story*
- *The different ways in which the story is told in the texts you have chosen.*

Point of view

The story is narrated by Alec Moore, 'an officer and a gentleman' who sits in his prison cell, awaiting death. Alec is quite a dispassionate person whose detachment allows him to tell us about the other characters in a reasonably objective way, which is not usual for a first person narrator. However, Alec is not an omniscient (all-seeing, all-knowing) narrator so we must, along with him, wonder about certain things. We never learn whether or not Alicia is telling the truth about Alec's parentage and we never learn how Alec's parents or Bennett react to his decision to defy both Major Glendinning and army regulations by shooting Jerry.

Alec does not seem to wish to portray himself in a particularly positive light, nor others in a particularly negative one. He is honest about himself and never denies that he is a somewhat weak man who lacks a natural sense of authority. As an officer, he is a failure. He admits that he is unable to 'control [the soldiers in his charge] nor give them comfort in any way'. This honesty has the effect of making us sympathise with Alec. When his mother and Major Glendinning berate him for what they perceive as his failings, he does not argue. Nor does Alec try to paint his mother or the major in a wholly negative light. Again, his natural sense of honesty and fairness come to the fore. He says that he may well be judging his mother unfairly when he criticises her, and he confesses that there were moments when he 'almost admired' Major Glendinning, this despite the fact that the major has sentenced him to death.

Social realism

How Many Miles to Babylon? is an example of social realism. It is an historically accurate depiction of the time in which the characters live. Alec represents the fading Anglo-Irish Ascendancy and Jerry represents the rising Irish nationalists. When the pair join the army and are sent to Flanders, we learn of the horrors of war at first hand. Whether Alec and Jerry are in Wicklow or Belgium, the society and the times in which they live have a major impact on their lives. Through Alec and Jerry's trials and tribulations we get an idea of the political and social issues of the time and the ways in which these issues impact on the young men's lives.

> Alec represents the fading Anglo-Irish Ascendancy and Jerry represents the rising Irish nationalists

Structure of the novel

The structure of *How Many Miles to Babylon?* is an interesting one. The book is circular; it begins and ends with Alec in his prison cell. We know from the outset that there is no hope for him and the flashbacks to his childhood and the series of events which have led to this sorry end only serve to draw us even deeper into the sad story of Alec's life to date. Alec tries to escape the misery of his family life but ends up being pulled into a downward spiral which eventually leads to his shooting his best friend dead and then being condemned to death himself. It is almost as if every effort Alec makes to escape the constraints of his unhappy life only lead to his being sucked into a faster, deeper whirlpool of misery. He flees the misery and the constraints of his home life only to find far more misery and constraint in his life as a soldier. The fact that the book begins and ends in the same place indicates that there is no escape. The circle never ends. Nobody breaks free. There is no happy ending. There is only death.

Symbols

Throughout the novel, swans are used as a symbol of grace, freedom and companionship. They are mentioned repeatedly and their presence seems to bring out the best in everyone, even Alicia. Alec's only mention of a surge of love for his mother is at the moment when he hears her gently urging the swans to return to the water. Swans also have a link to Irish mythology and poetry, of course. The Children of Lir are transformed into swans by their wicked stepmother, Aoife; and W.B. Yeats (whose poetry is referred to and quoted many times in the novel) turns to swans as a symbol of love, constancy and freedom in 'The Wild Swans at Coole'. So, it seems fitting that Alec and Jerry's story should be linked symbolically to swans.

> Alec's only mention of a surge of love for his mother is at the moment when he hears her gently urging the swans to return to the water

In *How Many Miles to Babylon?* the swans are associated with Jerry and Alec's relationship. Swans stay together for life, just as the friends plan to do. Like Alec and Jerry, the swans are happiest in their own element. When the birds are on land, they are awkward and ungainly. But in the lake they are graceful and free. Similarly, Alec and Jerry are happiest in and around the lake and the hills of their home place. The water is where they first meet properly and the last place in which they spend time together before joining the army. In this way, they are linked to the swans. This connection persists throughout the novel. When Jerry is in prison awaiting his sentence for going absent without leave, Alec sees a pair of swans flying overhead as he leads his men on a march. The grace, freedom and dignity of the swans is in stark contrast with the disorder and filth of the ragged lines of marching men below. Alec is both pleased and oddly embarrassed to see the swans flying overhead. They are a reminder of happier times in a better place. He raises a hand in greeting but just then the leading swan is shot down by one of his men. Alec is angry and dismayed but the men are unrepentant. Hardened by their time at the front and the sight of so much suffering and slaughter, they fail to see why the death of a bird should affect Alec so much. They cannot know the significance of the swans in Alec and Jerry's life.

The shooting of the swan foreshadows Jerry's death. Just as the swans are no longer a pair, so the young men's relationship is about to come to an abrupt end. Alec's inability to make his men see that what they have done is wrong emphasises his lack of authority. He tries to rebuke them but his voice is 'blown back' by the wind. Alec is unable to make his voice heard and even when he does manage to communicate his anger and dismay to the men, they are unmoved. Just as the shooting of the swan foreshadows Jerry's death, so do Alec's ineffectual protests foreshadow his powerlessness to move Major Glendinning when Jerry has been sentenced. The men's lack of respect for life mirrors the way in which all lives are cheap on the battlefields of Flanders.

Creation of characters

Alec lives in a world where people keep their feelings in check. They frown on open expressions of sentiment and emotion, believing such things to be the habits of the lower social classes. For the members of the upper classes, appearance is more important than reality. Jennifer Johnston's descriptions of Alicia Moore, in particular, are a wonderful example of creating a character through description. Alec tells us of her beauty, her impeccable manners and her exquisite clothes and jewellery. The contrast between the loveliness of Alicia's appearance and the ugliness of her nature is striking. On the night that she tells of Christopher Boyle's death, Alec watches as his mother reaches towards the fire for warmth. He notices the 'soft lace' falling around her hands and diamonds glittering on her fingers. It seems grotesque that such elegance and beauty should be linked to excited delight at the thought of a young man's death in the battlefields of Flanders. This juxtaposition of symbols of privilege and upper-class gentility alongside images of horror and death continues when Alec joins the army. Even at the front line, Major Glendinning keeps up the manners of polite society, bringing a lemon with him to slice into his tea. There is something dreadful about the fact that the major cuts the lemon with the same small, sharp knife which he uses to end the life of the screaming soldier in No Man's Land a short time later. This horror is compounded by the description of the major wiping the dead man's blood off the knife with 'an amazingly white handkerchief' in the same way that he had wiped the lemon juice from the blade earlier that evening.

> For the members of the upper classes, control and adherence to old values is more important than personal loyalty or love

For the members of the upper classes, control and adherence to old values is more important than personal loyalty or love. Alec's parents hate one another yet they keep up the appearance of a happy family by maintaining an elegant and well-run home, dressing perfectly, being excellent and generous hosts, engaging in all the correct social pursuits and never displaying emotion, particularly in front of the servants. Alec tells us that even when alone with one another, his parents 'never raised their voices, the words dropped malevolent and cool from their well-bred mouths'. In the same way, Major Glendinning despises what he calls 'wasteful emotions' and keeps his own in check as much as is possible. His speech is clipped and tightly controlled even at moments of great tension. When he is about to risk his life by going into No Man's Land to see what he can do for the screaming, dying soldier, Major Glendinning displays no fear or distress. His language is deliberately casual and he refers to the mission as an 'outing' to 'see to' the man. He is disgusted with Alec for failing to control his emotions in a similar manner and berates him angrily as soon as they are alone in their dug-out. The arrival of an enlisted man checks the major and, like the Moores in the presence of the servants, the major pretends all is well. Alec describes him as 'all affability, charming smiles'. Even in the midst of the horror and death at the front, the major believes that he must maintain his distance from the men and must keep up appearances.

Although they make every effort to control their emotions, Johnston manages to convey the hidden feelings of the upper-class characters through descriptions of their body language and in particular the movement of their hands. Throughout the novel there are repeated references to characters' hands betraying their thoughts. Alec says of his father that 'his voice would show little emotion but there were times when he would twist his hands together in a gesture of incredible violence'. At other times, such as on the morning of Alec's departure for the front, although Frederick Moore's voice may be calm and his words measured, his shaking hands betray his distress. Major Glendinning's self-control is shown by his hands, which Alec describes as lying still on the desk in front of him 'as if they were just two more of the inanimate objects that covered the surface'. Yet even the major is not immune to emotion, however much he may wish he were. Towards the end of the book his hands betray him by trembling after he strikes Alec for calling the army uniform 'some sort of fancy dress'.

'his voice would show little emotion but there were times when he would twist his hands together in a gesture of incredible violence'

Poetry, song and music

Poetry plays an important role in *How Many Miles to Babylon?* The title of the novel is taken from a children's nursery rhyme and it is the song that Alec sings shortly before his execution. That he should choose a children's nursery rhyme reminds us that Alec is little more than a boy in many ways and has been forced, like so many of his generation, to grow up far too quickly. The rhyme speaks of going on a journey and returning home, which of course Alec will never do now.

Alec often turns to poetry in moments of stress, particularly lines from Yeats. Major Glendinning regards such behaviour with distrust and is disgusted when Alec quotes lines from Yeats' 'The Secret Rose' during their mission of mercy into No Man's Land to see what can be done for the dying soldier. He tackles Alec about it when they return to the dug-out and Alec's explanation that 'it was more like an incantation … a sort of prayer' only angers the major further. He says that incantations and poetry are 'all the same' and that he has 'no time for the man who cannot face reality'.

Music and song feature throughout the novel and are a reflection of the differing social classes. Alicia plays the piano and arranges lessons for Alec, although these end when she takes a dislike to the tutor and insists that Frederick fire him. Jerry plays 'ballads, both sentimental and revolutionary' on his mouth organ and Alec attempts to sing along when he can. When Alicia hears Alec singing lines from 'The Croppy Boy' she is appalled. It is not the sort of song that one would expect a person of Alec's background to know. This song appears a number of times in the book and its subject matter is allied to the fate of Jerry and Alec. The song tells of an Irish rebel who is executed by the British. It is the song that Jerry sings in the moments leading up to his death. It is sad and chillingly appropriate that Jerry should sing the line 'Now Father bless me and let me go …' just before Alec shoots him dead.

General Vision and Viewpoint

Higher Level

Past questions on this mode of comparison have tended to focus on the following:

- *How the general vision and viewpoint of a text is determined by the success or failure of a character in his or her efforts to achieve fulfilment*
- *How you came to your understanding of the general vision and viewpoint in your chosen text*
- *The way in which a key moment or moments can influence your understanding of the general vision and viewpoint of a text*
- *How the general vision and viewpoint is shaped by the reader's feeling of optimism or pessimism in reading a text*
- *Your understanding of the general vision and viewpoint in your chosen text*
- *What you enjoyed about the general vision and viewpoint of your chosen text.*

How Many Miles to Babylon? is an almost overwhelmingly bleak novel. Jennifer Johnston presents us with a pessimistic vision of a young man who moves from a bad situation to a worse one and whose life seems to be on a downward spiral from the start. Alec has no future 'except what you can count in hours'. This depressing certainty hangs over Alec from the opening page and the reader is denied any opportunity to hope that things may yet end well.

The book opens on a grim note. Alec is sitting in a prison cell, awaiting execution. The setting echoes the pessimistic tone. Although Flanders may be 'the centre of the world for tens of thousands of men' it will also be 'the end of the world for many'. This prediction of Alec's underscores the hopelessness and futility that lie at the heart of the novel. The message we come away with is that all efforts are in vain. The world conspires to bring pain and misery to those who least deserve it. Even the weather reflects the mood of the text: Alec presumes that there is a 'thick and evil February rain' pouring down on the men as they attack the German lines. The pointlessness of the attack is highlighted by the linking of 'the heroes and the cowards, the masters and the slaves'. Regardless of their individual worth, all these men will die on the muddy fields of Flanders and there is no sense that they will have died for a noble cause or that their sacrifice will make the slightest difference to the war effort.

> Alec presumes that there is a 'thick and evil February rain' pouring down on the men as they attack the German lines

How Many Miles to Babylon? is not a book which deals with generalities but rather with the fate of individuals. Alec and Jerry's story is tragic but, because it is set against the backdrop of war, we are aware that such stories must be taking place all over the trenches. Even Major Glendinning acknowledges the level of sorrow and loss endured by the soldiers when he says, while denying Jerry compassionate leave, that Alec has never considered how many men in the British Expeditionary Force have 'fathers, brothers, sons, cousins missing, wounded, dead'. And yet the major insists that such pain must be ignored for the greater good of the war effort. There is something particularly horrifying about the fact that the major realises the suffering and the pain of his men yet still pushes them relentlessly and insists on treating them as parts of a machine rather than living, feeling individuals. It is little wonder that Alec, in the short time that is left before his execution, is glad that the major has not been to see him.

The army chaplain does visit Alec but Alec rejects his offers of consolation, saying that, far from offering anyone hope of an afterlife, priests seem to derive a satisfaction from making people 'afraid of death'. This adds greatly to the pessimistic tone of the novel. There seems to be no escape, no hope, no future for Alec. Even the chance of happiness in the next life is taken from him by a clergyman who says that Alec needs to consider his faith if he is to have any chance of being saved and who is distressed by Alec's 'frivolity' as he faces death.

Things do not get better as Alec looks back over his life and reflects on the series of events which have led him to this sorry end. He grows up in a deeply dysfunctional family. His parents loathe one another and the young Alec is little more than a pawn in their 'terrible game'. His mother uses him for her own ends and his ineffectual father is so isolated and unhappy that, despite his best efforts, he is unable to take control of his own life, let alone make his son's life better. This unhappy, insecure, loveless childhood presents us with a very bleak picture. Alec, constrained as he is by both family and social class, has little or no control over his own life. The description of his claustrophobic, stultifyingly dull life, from which there seems to be no hope of escape, ensures that the reader's expectations are soon as low as Alec's.

Alec's self-loathing and his lack of interest in his future adds to the bleak and pessimistic tone of the text. As Johnston has made him the narrator, Alec's voice naturally sets the tone for the novel. From the opening lines where he announces that he loves 'no living person' to the closing lines where he faces his death with equanimity, Alec shows no great interest in himself or in his future. There is a contrast between his imagined future and what he knows is the reality. He dreams of starting a racing yard with Jerry and seems full of specific plans in this regard, but at the same time he has little or no interest in his real future, which is running the Moore estate. His father does succeed in interesting him in this a little but it is never the dream that Alec turns to in times of stress. His real life is so bleak and largely loveless that he longs to escape from it. On the night before they leave to join the army, Alec even goes so far as to tell Jerry that he wishes to die. On the morning he leaves to enlist, Alec says: 'I abhor what I am doing. I abhor myself.' Joining the army does not give Alec any more reason to view his life more optimistically. Even his daydreams of the future

> Alec's self-loathing and his lack of interest in his future adds to the bleak and pessimistic tone of the text

offer little hope. Towards the end of the novel, when Jerry returns after having gone absent without leave, the pair discuss their future lives. Alec states clearly that he does not wish to marry or to live with anyone else, even Jerry. He has no wish to be part of the world and only wants to live alone. He says that he is 'only afraid' when he is with other people. Life has taught Alec that closeness with others brings misery and pain and he reacts by wishing nothing more than to remove himself from such misery, either through death or self-imposed isolation.

'I abhor what I am doing. I abhor myself'

In times of great stress both Alec and Jerry turn to their memories of their childhood in County Wicklow. They think back to their time on the lake and to the swans which swam there. Swans are a symbol of hope, freedom and love in the novel. They are mentioned repeatedly and their presence seems to bring out the best in everyone, even Alicia. Alec's only mention of a surge of love for his mother is at the moment when he hears her gently urging the swans to return to the water. Swans also have a link to Irish mythology and poetry, of course. The Children of Lir are transformed into swans by their wicked stepmother, Aoife; and W.B. Yeats (whose poetry is referred to and quoted many times in the novel) turns to swans as a metaphor for love, constancy and freedom in 'The Wild Swans at Coole'. So, it seems fitting that Alec and Jerry's story should be linked symbolically to swans.

Even this glimmer of hope and optimism is taken away at the end of the novel, however. As Jerry faces death, he finds that he cannot turn to those consoling memories of the past. He claims that he 'can remember nothing'. Alec urges him to think of the swans but Jerry replies that the memory of the crack of their wings sounds 'like gun shots'. Even the memory of the swans has been corrupted by the horrific experience of war. The evil of war has all but consumed the young men and driven them to despair. There seems nothing left for them to cling to in their hour of need.

It could be argued that Alec achieves a measure of success in that he thwarts the plans of his mother and Major Glendinning by shooting Jerry and accepting the inevitable consequence, his own execution by firing squad. However, this success is limited. The message seems to be that the only way to escape the grimness and the unfairness of this life is to choose death. Alec may have frustrated the plans of his mother and Major Glendinning, but he paid the ultimate price. That Alec should face his death calmly and dispassionately shows us that he sees no point in living. There could hardly be a more bleak vision and viewpoint than this.

The other message that comes through from this novel is that love is not enough. Even those who care deeply about us cannot save us. Frederick and Alec care for one another but are unable either to express this feeling plainly or to save one another from Alicia's determination to prevent their happiness. Alec's powerlessness to save Jerry is highlighted in the final pages of the novel. As readers, we share in Alec's horror and desperation as he realises that there is nothing he can do to prevent Jerry's death. His decision to take matters into his own hands and shoot Jerry himself is a merciful act but it does not hide the awful truth, that this life is cruel and harsh and that evil ultimately triumphs over good.

The only real note of hope at any stage in Alec's unhappy life is his relationship with Jerry. The other relationships in the novel are not positive models for the young Alec and leave him determined to live alone and in a house that is only 'a shell' for his body. He is so emotionally scarred and damaged by his parents' miserable marriage that he thinks the only hope of any sort of peace in this life lies in detachment and distance. His father reinforces this by telling Alec how dreadful it is to be married to someone who is indifferent to you. Frederick Moore loves his son but is not capable of parenting him successfully or of being a positive role model for him. Jerry's friendship alone shows Alec that closeness with another person need not mean pain or hurt. At least, that is how it begins. But as soon as others learn of the friendship, they conspire to separate the friends. The world in which Alec lives is portrayed as a hostile place peopled by selfish, weak or cruel individuals who place their own concerns above Alec's. Jerry is an exception to the rule, but the ending of the novel shows that love is not enough. This is a bleak and incredibly pessimistic message and leaves the reader almost as heartbroken and despairing as Alec.

The book ends where it began, with Alec alone in prison, awaiting execution. This circularity reflects Alec's own view that there are 'eternal recurrences' that 'weave and unweave themselves endlessly through life and history'. Man, he seems to be saying, is powerless. Some greater force controls our destiny and there is nothing we can do to escape our fate. Alec does not suppose that he will ever be able to change the way of the world; he simply wishes to be able to 'see the world with clarity'. As it is, it seems a confusing and inexplicably hostile place and Alec's only defence is to withdraw from it whenever he can. His desire to stay detached from all that happens about him increases as the novel progresses but his ability to do so is undermined by his relationship with Jerry. Much as he wishes that he did not care for anyone, Alec cares for Jerry and in the end sees no option but to permanently remove his friend and himself from this grim world.

Cultural Context

Higher Level

Social Setting

Ordinary Level

Past questions on these modes of comparison have tended to focus on the following:

Higher Level

- *The way in which the world or culture the characters inhabit affects the storyline*
- *The way in which the world or culture they inhabit shapes the characters' attitudes and values*
- *What is interesting about the world or culture of the texts*
- *How the author establishes the cultural context.*

Ordinary Level

- *What you liked or disliked about the social setting*
- *What you found interesting about the social setting*
- *The way in which the social setting influences the characters*
- *How a key moment can show us the way in which the social setting affects the characters.*

Political background

How Many Miles to Babylon? is set in a time of great political upheaval in Ireland and Europe. The situation in Ireland is becoming ever more restless as opposition to British rule grows. Even within the groups opposed to British rule, there is division. Some believe that Home Rule is the answer and they are content to allow Ireland to remain a part of the British empire but to be allowed self-governance. Others feel that this does not go far enough and want complete independence, achieved by violent means if necessary. In the northern counties, the majority want neither independence nor Home Rule and are busily arming themselves for what they see as the inevitable conflict. In the southern counties, those in favour of Home Rule and independence are also arming themselves against what they perceive as the threat from the Ulster Volunteers. The country looks to be on the brink of civil war but then war breaks out in Europe and the issue of Home Rule is put aside until peace is restored.

This turmoil and confusion has a powerful effect on the characters' lives. Each of the main characters represents a different political viewpoint.

Jerry Crowe is against Home Rule and wants Ireland to become fully independent. He believes that the fight for freedom is imminent and part of the reason he enlists in the British army is to become a trained soldier so that he can play a valuable role in the coming struggle.

Alicia Moore has no time for those who want an independent Ireland. She suspects Jerry may be a member of what she calls 'a criminal organisation' and uses this as another reason why she wants Alec to break off all contact with his childhood friend. Like Major Glendinning, Alicia Moore disapproves of any Irish person who seeks independence from Britain and she calls such an attitude 'a dangerous disaffection'. At the same time, there is little sign that she is particularly interested in the war in Europe. She is only concerned about the ways in which she can use that war to serve her own ends.

> Jerry Crowe is against Home Rule and wants Ireland to become fully independent

Like Alicia Moore, Major Glendinning clings to the old ways and has no time for those who want a free Ireland. He asks Alec if he is 'tainted with the Irish disease' of disaffection and disloyalty. For the major, obedience to king and country is of paramount importance. He thinks those Irish soldiers who want a free Ireland might also be traitors who could pass on valuable intelligence to the Germans. The war is all that matters to Major Glendinning and he is willing to do whatever it takes to ensure that the men under his command are efficient soldiers.

Frederick Moore thinks that Irish independence will become a reality sooner or later and he seems to sympathise with the cause. He considers himself one of those who took the land from the people and he says he feels a responsibility to keep it well so that 'it will, when the moment comes, be handed back in good order'. He does not appear to admire the British government, saying at one stage that their decision not to introduce conscription in Ireland proves that 'for once the British aren't being complete fools'. He has no real interest in the war in Europe, saying that he feels 'remote' and 'protected' in his home in Wicklow.

Bennett does not appear to take Irish independence terribly seriously. He is interested in Jerry's talk of a free Ireland and claims to be a 'fellow revolutionary' but it is doubtful that he really means what he says. His tone is flippant and he refers to Padraig Pearse as Jerry's 'Mr Whatsit'. Bennett gives the impression that he enjoys theoretical discussion but doesn't believe that anything will

'for once the British aren't being complete fools'

really come of an Irish rebellion. His attitude towards the war is equally irreverent. He thinks that the British and German governments treat their soldiers like performing dogs and he appears contemptuous of the 'fat men at home' who determine the soldiers' fate. For all his talk, however, Bennett does not rebel against authority beyond borrowing a few horses for a spin in the countryside. When the major who catches them out riding accuses Bennett of not taking the war seriously, Bennett is shocked.

At the end of the day, Bennett is a young conservative who appears to be flirting with the idea of abandoning the old ways but at the same time is keen to be one of the 'whip crackers'. Bennett's views are not easy to define and perhaps he represents the less hardline members of the younger generation of Englishmen in the early years of the twentieth century.

Alec Moore is not sure what to think. He represents those who are confused by the differing political viewpoints and who are horrified at the thought of another war, this time on Irish soil. Alec is a product of an Anglo-Irish upbringing and he is not sure which side, if any, he supports. Jerry tells Bennett that Alec 'doesn't know if he's coming or going. He's been brought up to trust the British.' Bennett, for his part, tells Alec that 'you attach the adjective "English" to anything you don't like'. Alec is uncertain and unwilling to commit to any side in the debate, preferring to change the subject to more pleasant matters whenever possible.

> Alec is a product of an Anglo-Irish upbringing and he is not sure which side, if any, he supports

Alec has no interest in the war in Europe. He does not wish to fight and only does so in the end because his mother makes it impossible for him to remain at home any longer. Alec does not believe that the army should view the soldiers as a type of expendable livestock and his dislike of the war grows more intense as he sees the effect it has on those around him.

There is nothing glorious or noble about war as it is depicted in this novel. Jennifer Johnston shows us the suffering endured by the men at the front and the impression we are left with is that war is futile and inhumane. The account of the soldier dying slowly in No Man's Land is particularly horrific.

It is not just the constant threat of being shot or shelled that makes life at the front so dreadful, it is also the appalling conditions in which the men live. The descriptions of the rats, the mud, the dead bodies all around and the soldiers' rapidly deteriorating health makes it easy to understand why so many men died in the trenches without ever being involved in any fighting.

It is by showing us the varying political viewpoints of the main characters that Jennifer Johnston succeeds in interesting us in this aspect of the cultural context/social setting. We see the reality of war and of political upheaval and we understand the effect it has on the lives of individuals.

Setting

There is a strong contrast between the rolling hills of County Wicklow and the war-torn fields of Flanders. The Moores' family home, with all its finery, family portraits, mounted antlers and various symbols of wealth and status in Ascendancy Ireland, is described in detail. Like his father, Alec feels an affinity for the land and for his ancestral home, and is delighted to return to it after his four months in Europe with Alicia. As he works with his father on estate business, Alec slowly comes to the realisation that the land will be his one day. He is struck one evening by the thought that, like his father, he will sit in the old chair in the drawing room as generations of his family have done before him. This gradual increasing of Alec's tie to the family estate has not gone unnoticed by Alicia and she is quick to break Alec's connection to his home place when she sees that Alec wants to remain there rather than going to war. When she tells him that Frederick is not his father, Alec is crushed. One of the reasons for his shock and dismay is that he now feels adrift. He is 'dispossessed in a sentence' and later says that he now feels like 'an intruder' as he passes the Moore family portraits on the walls.

Jerry shares Alec's love of the land, and on the night before they leave to join the army, Jerry stands staring at the lake and the hills, trying to fix the memory of them in his mind so that he can 'bring it out and look at it' during bad times. Neither Jerry nor Alec may have had as many opportunities in their lives as they would have wished but at least they had a beautiful place in which to spend their snatched moments of happiness.

For both young men the setting in which they grow up plays an important role in their lives but it is all too quickly replaced by the horror and desolation of the battlefields of Flanders. The descriptions of this place are hellish. In the opening pages of the novel, Alec describes the scene where the latest battle is being fought as 'a hundred yards of mournful earth' where many men will soon die. Even the weather seems to conspire against the men; Alec feels certain that there is a 'thick and evil February rain' falling on them as they advance on the front.

Compared to the luxury of the Moores' house or even the rural beauty of the land where Jerry worked, the fields of Flanders and the farmhouse at West Outre are cold, miserable, rat-infested, wet and horrifically uncomfortable. It seems that Alec and Jerry have escaped one restrictive setting only to find themselves in another which is infinitely worse.

Class distinction

The class distinctions in this novel are mainly those between the Anglo-Irish Ascendancy and the Irish labouring classes. The novel is set in a time when the balance of power rests with members of the Ascendancy like the Moores, but change is coming. The old order is about to give way to the new. Some people, such as Jerry, embrace the possibility of change while others, such as Alicia, resist the very idea of it. Frederick Moore knows that the landed gentry are likely to lose their influence and power but he does not seem unduly concerned about it.

Alec Moore is one of the Protestant Ascendancy but, to his mother's annoyance, he refuses to fully embrace the Ascendancy's values and seems not to care about his social position. Alicia herself is keenly conscious of her position in society and makes every effort to maintain her attitude of superiority over those from a lower social class. Her clothes, manner and language mark her out as someone from a privileged background and she is determined to maintain an air of superiority at all times. Alec's friendship with Jerry offends Alicia and she tries, in vain, to impress upon Alec that such associations are not the done thing. Her snobbery is almost comical at times, particularly when she suspects that Alec may have been discussing the threat of war with the servants. Her voice rises 'to a slight gasp' as she contemplates the horror inherent in her son conversing with such lowly people. She is not any happier to discover that it is Jerry who is the source of Alec's new-found knowledge and angrily repeats that the friendship must end immediately.

Alec does not care about his social position and it means nothing to him that Jerry is from a poor family. However, although he may not care

> The old order is about to give way to the new. Some people, such as Jerry, embrace the possibility of change while others, such as Alicia, resist the very idea of it

about class distinctions, that does not mean Alec is not aware of them. He is grateful when Bennett treats Jerry with courtesy even though Jerry is not an officer and not from the same social class as Bennett. To Alec, the wealth and privilege that comes with being a member of the Ascendancy is not a benefit, but rather an obstacle which prevents him from doing what he wants in life.

Jerry Crowe is well aware of the difficulties of befriending someone from a different social class. He knows that not only Alec's family, but his own, too, will object to the friendship and see it as unsuitable. However, like Alec, Jerry is perfectly willing to put class differences aside in the name of friendship.

> The snobbery and injustice associated with the class system follow them all the way to the fields of Flanders

Neither Jerry nor Alec can call their lives their own. They are bound by social structures which determine their circle of friends, their educational opportunities and their financial status. Jerry must leave school early and earn money to support his family. Whether he wanted a higher level of education or not, such an option was not on the cards for him. Alec, on the other hand, may have the benefits of money and a good academic education, but he is forced to live a lonely, isolated life in the Big House. He is not permitted to mix with the local boys and when his friendship with Jerry is discovered, his parents put a stop to it.

Neither Alec nor Jerry succeed in escaping the class barriers that come between them. The snobbery and injustice of the class system follow them all the way to the fields of Flanders. As Jerry had predicted, Alec is made an officer because of his upper-class background, while Jerry is an ordinary enlisted man. Major Glendinning assumes Alicia Moore's role and does his best to prevent Alec from fraternising with Jerry. He is disgusted that Alec even speaks to Jerry and insists that he will have 'no talking between the men and the officers'. Like Alicia, Major Glendinning despises the peasant Irish and believes they are untrustworthy and potentially dangerous. When Jerry goes absent without leave, the major suspects that he may be a traitor and could even be passing military intelligence to the enemy.

Religion

One of the reasons Major Glendinning gives for distrusting the Irish soldiers in his charge is their religious beliefs. He is suspicious of Catholics and asks Alec what his religious beliefs are after the incident in which he, the major, has ended the life of the screaming soldier in No Man's Land. Alec had quoted a line from a poem by Yeats and the major, not recognising it, assumed it was a prayer. He is contemptuous of what he calls Catholic 'incantations' and claims that they are merely another way for men to avoid facing reality. Catholicism is allied with overly emotional and potentially rebellious behaviour and is yet another reason for those in power to wish to separate Alec and Jerry.

Power

Power, in *How Many Miles to Babylon?*, rests firmly in the hands of the less appealing characters. Society may be on the brink of change and the dispossessed may be braced for rebellion, but this potential is still unfulfilled by the time the novel ends. The world of the text, therefore, is one in which the weak perish and the strong survive. Good does not triumph over evil; in fact the opposite is true. Alec Moore, Frederick Moore and Jerry Crowe are kind, decent men who want to do the best for those they love. However, they are thwarted in this by stronger, more ruthless characters. Alicia Moore and Major Glendinning represent the callous, selfish face of authority and power. They use the gentler characters for their own purposes and discard them the moment they have outlived their usefulness.

> At the end of the novel, Alec takes some measure of power into his own hands by flouting authority and doing what he feels is right

At the end of the novel, Alec takes some measure of power into his own hands by flouting authority and doing what he feels is right. While his mother and Major Glendinning will certainly disapprove of his decision, he has at least learned one lesson from them: that people should do what they feel is best, regardless of how that affects those around them. Alicia Moore and Major Glendinning always wanted Alec to be a stronger, more decisive man.

What they really wanted, of course, was that he would strongly and decisively support their opinions. Alec's decision to end Jerry's life is a brave, selfless one, but one which will undoubtedly earn him little respect from his mother or his commanding officer.

Family

The portrayal of family life in *How Many Miles to Babylon?* is a very negative one. Alec has an unhappy, lonely childhood during which he is caught in the middle of his parents' failed marriage. They hate one another and, as Alec says 'their only meeting place was the child'. Alec grows up believing that he is the sole reason his parents tolerate one another. This is a heavy burden for any young boy to bear and his mother does little or nothing to make him believe otherwise. Indeed, she points out to him on the night before his departure for the war that she has sacrificed any chance she may have had of a happy life in order to raise Alec in a stable family setting. The irony of this escapes her. Alec could hardly have been unhappier or more lonely had he been raised in a less conventional family environment. Indeed, he would probably have been far happier being raised by one contented parent than by two miserable ones.

Alicia shows no maternal instinct and uses Alec for her own purposes. She has no interest in her son beyond his usefulness to her and she hopes he may grow up to be the companion to her that her husband cannot be. When Alec proves a disappointment to Alicia, she packs him off to the war in a final act of selfishness.

Frederick Moore is a kindly but weak man who is unable to stand up to his domineering wife. Alec's loneliness and lack of a normal upbringing does not escape his father's notice but when he tries to remedy the situation by sending the boy away to school, Alec's mother vetoes the suggestion as she does not want to be left alone with her husband.

The effect of all of this on Alec is to turn him into a solitary, unhappy boy. He may have wealth and privilege, but he does not have a loving family. When he meets Jerry, Alec is pathetically delighted to have a friend. Jerry provides Alec with much of what has been missing in his life to date and the friendship assumes a greater importance in Alec's life than it might have done if he had been raised in a normal, loving family.

We do not know as much about Jerry's family as we do about Alec's, but what we do know is not particularly positive. Jerry's father is largely absent as he is a soldier in the British army, but when he is home, he does nothing to contribute to family life. Jerry admits that he hardly knows his father, and what he does know, he fears. Mr Crowe is 'rare and quick with the fist' and Jerry says that the only way to cope is always to show him 'a brave face'.

Jerry's mother is keen for Jerry to become a soldier to earn money for her. Like Alicia Moore, she does not seem unduly concerned about her son's fate in the war. When Jerry's father goes missing, Mrs Moore writes to her son asking him to find out what happened to her husband. The tone of her letter is self-pitying. She shows no real interest in Jerry or his father beyond their ability to provide her with a regular income.

> The relationship between Jerry and Alec is like that between brothers. This is particularly true of Alec, who lacks almost all contact with youngsters of his own age

Jerry, like Alec, has no strong ties to home or to family. Instead, he focuses on a dream and a friendship. This is what Alec does too and the closeness of the pair is revealed in their planning of the racing stable they will one day run. This vision is a consolation and a refuge for both of them. Initially, it seems Alec is the one who relies on it most but at the end of his life Jerry talks about 'all those race courses our horses would have won at'.

The relationship between Jerry and Alec is like that between brothers. This is particularly true of Alec, who lacks almost all contact with youngsters of his own age. Jerry is the closest thing he will ever have to a sibling. From the earliest days when they wrestle and play to their attempts to do the best for one another in war-torn Belgium, the young men's affection and fellowship remain at the heart of this story.

Theme or Issue

Higher Level and Ordinary Level

Past questions on this mode of comparison have tended to focus on the following:

Higher Level

- *What insights you gained from studying the theme*
- *How the study of a particular text changed or reinforced your view of the theme*
- *The way in which key moments can heighten your awareness of a particular theme*
- *How the presentation of the theme can add to the impact of the text*
- *How the theme helps to maintain your interest in the text.*

Ordinary Level

- *What you learned about your chosen theme*
- *How a key moment in the text reveals the theme*
- *Why you feel that the theme made the text interesting*
- *How the theme is presented in the text*
- *How the theme plays an important role in the story*
- *How the theme affects the life of a character in the text.*

Theme or Issue: escape

Alec Moore is a lonely young man who longs to escape the crushing weight of his mother's expectations and society's expectations of him. Unfortunately, Alec's attempt to escape is a failure. We know this from the opening pages of the book when he explains that he has been sentenced to be shot by firing squad the next morning and only has a short time left to live. His recollections of his life to date show us clearly that this tragic end is simply the final chapter in a life that has been gradually and inexorably crushing Alec's spirit until he is left with no option but to seek the only way out that remains open to him: his own death.

Alec's home life is suffocating and miserable. His parents are locked in a dysfunctional marriage from which there is no escape. Divorce is not an option for people of their social standing and it is unlikely in any case that Alicia would be willing to forego the trappings of wealth in order to achieve a measure of personal liberty. His parents' misery affects Alec in a number of different ways. On a practical level, it restricts his freedom by ensuring that he remains at home rather than go to school. Alicia is determined not to be left alone in the house with Frederick and keeps Alec at home to act as a barrier between them. He is a pawn in their 'terrible game'. Lonely and friendless, the little boy is forced to spend his free time either with his bitterly unhappy parents or alone in his schoolroom.

> Lonely and friendless, the little boy is forced to spend his free time either with his bitterly unhappy parents or alone in his schoolroom

From early childhood onwards, Alec is restricted by the social class into which he is born. He may have wealth and privilege but he sees his membership of the Ascendancy as a barrier to happiness rather than an advantage. Whenever his position in society is mentioned to him, it is done in such a way as to make him aware that he is not free to behave as he likes but must instead conform to the social mores of his class. His parents' reaction to the discovery of his friendship with Jerry is an example of this. No matter how lonely and miserable young Alec may be, his parents view his social standing as more important than his personal happiness, and tell him that he must not see Jerry again. Alicia's manner as she says this is imperious and inflexible: 'You are never to see him again.' Frederick at least tries to explain his decision by telling Alec that he must accept the 'sad fact' that the friendship must end because of the 'responsibilities and limitations of the class' to which Alec belongs. Frederick's gentler explanation is no better than Alicia's harsh one, however. Both parents are agreed that Alec must end the only relationship which has brought him joy. It is no wonder that Alec should want to escape this life, which seems to offer nothing but instead threatens to take away the one thing he values above all others.

As there seems little practical chance of Alec's getting away from his family, he escapes instead into the dream of a perfect future. He imagines that he and Jerry will set up a racing yard together. Jerry is more realistic and has, unlike Alec, thought about the fact that Alec is the heir to his family's estate and is therefore tied to it for life. Alec has not given this any consideration, possibly because to think of it would be to acknowledge to himself that his entire life is mapped out for him and that there is no prospect of his having any control over his future. He focuses instead on the dream of the racing stables he and Jerry will run and this vision sustains him whenever he feels unhappy.

Despite Alicia's destructive influence, Alec does at one stage begin to find some measure of happiness in his home life. In an effort to distract his son from the 'unsuitable relationship' with Jerry, Frederick Moore takes Alec under his wing and begins to educate him in the ways of estate management. As father and son spend time together they become closer, a fact which does not go unnoticed by Alicia. Alec notes that it 'angered her more and more as the months passed, to watch the mutual pleasure given and received between my father and myself'. Having insisted that Alec stay at home when Frederick wanted him to go off to school, Alicia now changes tack abruptly and decides that she wants Alec to join the army. Her motives are purely selfish: she wants the vicarious glory that comes with being the mother of an heroic soldier and she wants to deprive her husband of his son. Alec is reluctant to leave the land he loves and the father to whom he has grown close, but Alicia cruelly

'angered her more and more as the months passed, to watch the mutual pleasure given and received between my father and myself'

tells him that he is not Frederick's son. Alec is appalled to be 'dispossessed in a sentence' and flees the house, ending up at the village dance at the crossroads. He meets Jerry and, on hearing that his childhood friend is enlisting the following day, decides that he will join up with him.

Alec's failure to escape is horrifyingly clear when he joins the army and replaces one restrictive, controlling, uncaring situation with another. Alicia Moore may have driven Alec away but he only succeeds in placing himself under the authority of someone infinitely more controlling and with far more power than Alicia. The similarities between Major Glendinning and Alicia Moore are chilling and add to our feeling of hopelessness when we consider Alec's situation. Like Alicia, Major Glendinning disapproves of Alec's friendship with

> The similarities between Major Glendinning and Alicia Moore are chilling and add to our feeling of hopelessness when we consider Alec's situation

Jerry and, again like Alicia, he is determined to mould Alec into the sort of man he wants and needs. The major's mannerisms even mirror those of Alicia Moore. He places importance on the ceremony around having a cup of tea, for example. He brings a lemon with him and slices it daintily into his tea. This may not seem important but it is reminiscent of Alicia's tea drinking ceremonies with 'china tea in thin cups, a ring of lemon floating on the pale liquid', and it reminds the reader that Alec has replaced his mother with an authority figure who is equally concerned with appearances and the correct way of doing things rather than the happiness of the individual. Like Alicia, the major calls Alec 'obtuse' and makes every effort to force Alec to become the sort of officer he approves of. The uncanny similarities between Alicia and Major Glendinning continue throughout the text and reinforce the fact that Alec has not escaped at all. His life is still not his own.

If Alec had thought that by joining the army with Jerry he would have greater opportunities to renew their friendship, he is soon disillusioned. Not only are the men separated by their social class but they are now also separated by rank. And Major Glendinning proves a far greater threat to Alec and Jerry's friendship than Alicia Moore ever was. The major has the power of life and death over his men and drives this point home frequently in his conversations with them. Alec's personal freedom is as curtailed as it ever was at home and he has virtually no say over how he spends his time or with whom he spends it. At least in Wicklow he and Jerry could escape to the hills behind the house and be reasonably sure that nobody would see them or report their meetings to Alicia and Frederick. In Flanders, there is no such hope of privacy. Bennett does manage to secure some horses and the three men go riding across the Belgian countryside but they are seen and their activities reported to Major Glendinning. The major takes Alec aside and tells him that he will not tolerate any deviation from the strict code of discipline that he expects his soldiers to obey at all times.

Alec's reaction to Major Glendinning's attempts to change him and to control his life is much the same as his reaction when Alicia tried to do the same thing. He rarely openly rebels but he persists in his own beliefs with a sort of quiet stubbornness. Whenever he gets the chance to meet up with Jerry, Alec does so. These opportunities do not come very often and Major Glendinning always seems to be lurking close by, ready to put a stop to the fraternising of which he so strongly disapproves.

> His fear is not so much of death but of some day accepting the 'grotesque obscenity' all around him

Life in Flanders becomes ever more hellish as time passes. Alec admits to being frightened almost all the time and he even finds it difficult to find refuge in his dreams. His fear is not so much of death but of some day accepting the 'grotesque obscenity' all around him. Alec is still determined to maintain some degree of control over his own thoughts, at least, and he finds a way to partially escape the horror that surrounds him by retreating into himself and concentrating on his own 'petty discomforts and indispositions to the exclusion of everything else except the bare bones of duty'.

Jerry does manage to evade those in charge for long enough to go in search of the truth about his missing father. However, he returns to the farmhouse at West Outre, to Alec's dismay. He knows that Major

Glendinning will have Jerry tried for desertion in the face of enemy fire and he is desperate to save his friend. Jerry thinks there is little point as he believes the war is now so widespread that there is nowhere left to run.

Alec and Jerry have been pushed to a place from which there is no way back. Jerry is sentenced to death for desertion and Alec is ordered to take charge of the firing squad. Realising that there is nothing he can do to avoid the inevitable death of the only person he has ever truly loved, Alec decides to shoot Jerry himself and spare his friend the agonising wait until his execution. In this way, Alec does gain some measure of control over his life and he does succeed in denying his mother and Major Glendinning the satisfaction of turning him into the sort of man they think he should be, but he pays a terrible price for this partial freedom. He gives Jerry a fast and merciful death but he now faces the same fate as his friend. Nobody is left to save Alec and he sits and waits alone. He is remarkably calm in the face of his impending death. There is nothing left to tie him to this world now that Jerry is dead. Nobody can hurt Alec now, and to that extent, at least, he has at last escaped.

Relationships

Ordinary Level or as a ***Theme Option*** for Higher Level

Past questions on Relationships (Ordinary Level) have tended to focus on the following:

- *Why you find the relationship to be complicated*
- *Why you consider the relationship to be successful*
- *Why you consider the relationship to be a failure*
- *Why the relationship made a strong impression on you.*

Alec and Jerry have been aware of one another for quite a while before they ever meet properly. Alec, a keen observer, has noticed Jerry's obvious poverty but also his clever, confident way of keeping clear of horses' hooves and quick-tempered men. Although they never speak and barely exchange an occasional nod, Alec knows that Jerry is keenly aware of him too and every bit as interested in the son of the Big House as he is in the horses.

The first meaningful encounter between the two boys takes place at the lake. Jerry is confident and at home in the lake, despite that fact that he is trespassing. He invites Alec in for a swim as if he, Jerry, were the landowner. When Alec says that he could have Jerry prosecuted for trespassing, Jerry is completely unmoved by the rather weak threat. Jerry's self-assured, relaxed manner contrasts sharply with Alec's rather cautious approach to new or unexpected situations.

Alec is intrigued by Jerry. The boys have very little in common apart from their similarity in age but the differences just make each seem more interesting to the other. Alec, denied normal contact with siblings or friends of his own age, is fascinated by Jerry's easy ways and worldly-wise attitude. Nor does Jerry seem in the slightest bit fazed by Alec's superior social position. Jerry suggests a bargain: he will teach

Alec to fight if Alec teaches him to ride. This is significant as it is only in his relationship with Jerry that Alec enjoys any sort of equality. Jerry sees Alec as someone with something to offer. To most other people, Alec is something of a disappointment. He does not measure up to anyone's expectations and is seen as a failure by all those around him, with the possible exception of his father. But even there, Frederick notes that Alec is, like him, a weak man who will obey Alicia's orders however much he dislikes them. Frederick may love his son, but he sees in him a reflection of himself, and as his own life is filled with misery, loneliness and disappointment, it is unlikely that he is entirely satisfied with the way his son has turned out. Jerry is the only one who sees Alec as a person with something to give and yet he does not make any great demands on him. He simply treats him as a friend, and the bargain they strike means that both benefit from the relationship.

'a great one for thinking things will be easy'

Alec responds to Jerry's open, straightforward approach with delight. He teaches Jerry to ride and Jerry keeps his end of the bargain by teaching Alec to fight. The pair spend many happy days together in the hills behind the house. Alec dreams that they will have a racing yard together some day. In his mind, this offers the perfect solution to their problems; they can work side by side and be partners. Jerry laughs when Alec suggests this, saying that Alec is 'a great one for thinking things will be easy'. Still, he goes along with Alec's idea and the pair plan their future happily.

Although the boys enjoy their time together, it is clear from the outset that there are external forces which threaten their relationship. Both Alec and Jerry are aware that their families would try to put a stop to the friendship were they to hear of it and so Alec refers to Jerry as his 'secret friend'. He knows that he can never visit Jerry in his house, nor can Jerry visit him in the Big House. At the same time, Alec is not as aware of the difficulties of the pair remaining friends as Jerry is. Jerry knows that Alec is the heir to the estate and he has thought about that, asking Alec what he will do with his inheritance when the time comes. Alec has never given any consideration to his future as master of the Big House, preferring instead to cling to the dream of starting a racing yard with Jerry. There is also the threat of an Irish uprising and a war in Europe. Jerry, although the same age as Alec, is more aware of the political situation and tells Alec that the British will go to war soon to 'fix the Germans' and that the Irish, in turn, 'are going to fix the British'. Alec accuses him of dreaming, which is ironic, as Jerry is talking about a very likely future while Alec is the one holding on to a dream. Still, although these threats hang over the boys' relationship, they continue to meet and ride their horses together whenever they get the chance.

The easy friendship of childhood also changes slightly when Jerry has to leave school and get a job in order to help support his family. Alec, clearly worried that he might lose his friend and wanting to help out in some way, suggests that Jerry should apply for a job in the Moores' stables, but Jerry refuses. He, unlike Alec, is acutely aware of the class differences between the pair and knows that if he were to work directly for Alec's family, everything 'would be different'. Alec's life is a static, sheltered one and he does not have Jerry's experience of the ways of the world. Jerry realises that neither his family nor Alec's would tolerate the friendship between the two and that if he were to take a job working for the Moores, it would turn his relationship with Alec into one of a master and a servant. This would be uncomfortable for Jerry and it would make the difference between the pair all too obvious. Those who might have been willing to turn a blind eye to their association would be even less likely to do so if Jerry were Alec's employee. It is a sign of Jerry's affection for his friend that he refuses to take a job which would undoubtedly suit him far better than working as a farm hand. Jerry does not want to profit from his

> Jerry realises that neither his family nor Alec's would tolerate the friendship between the two and that if he were to take a job working for the Moores, it would turn his relationship with Alec into one of a master and a servant

friendship with Alec. His friendship comes with no strings attached and he prefers to keep it that way.

Inevitably, Alec and Jerry's friendship is discovered. Alicia is horrified, and insists that Alec instantly break all connections with Jerry, who she refers to disparagingly as 'that boy'. Alec tries to protest but is not strong enough to stand up to his mother. She and Frederick tell Alec that he must stop seeing Jerry. Their approaches differ; Alicia speaks in imperatives while Frederick tries to explain to his son that, although it is 'a sad fact' that their differing backgrounds make the friendship unsuitable, Alec must accept 'the responsibilities and limitations' of his class. Alicia takes Alec off to tour Europe. When they return, it is autumn. Frederick begins to teach Alec about the running of the estate and manages to keep his son so busy that it is not until the following spring that he sees Jerry 'at close quarters' again. When he does, the difference between them is obvious. Jerry has won the local point-to-point and is receiving his prize from Frederick Moore. There is a clear distinction between the 'polite clapping of the ladies and gentlemen standing round' and the 'wild cheer from outside the fence'. The fence is a literal and a metaphorical barrier between the villagers and the local gentry. Alec and Jerry each represent their own class as they face each other for the first time in many months. Alec is embarrassed to see that his childhood friend is wearing a pair of his cast-off breeches. Jerry, for his part, is equally disconcerted to meet Alec under these circumstances and accepts Alec's congratulations awkwardly and without looking him in the eye. He thanks Alec, but calls him 'sir'. It is not until Alec breaks the ice by honestly and enthusiastically complimenting Jerry's horse that the tension is dissipated and Jerry begins to chat to Alec with something like his old animation. Alec reaches out a hand to Jerry and is obviously on the brink of explaining his absence and suggesting that they meet again. However, Alicia Moore almost immediately intervenes, dragging Alec away and telling him furiously that he is to have nothing more to do with 'that young man'.

It seems as if Alec and Jerry's relationship is unlikely to continue if

Alec's mother has her way. However, it is her decision to send Alec off to join the army that brings the two young men together again. Alicia's cruelty on the night before Alec joins the army drives a distraught and bewildered Alec from the house. Hearing music, he follows the sound until he comes to the crossroads where a village dance is in full swing. Jerry spots his old friend and offers him a drink. They chat and reminisce and fall into their old ways again. Jerry tells Alec that he is enlisting the following morning and Alec says that he is, too.

For all that their lives have changed, the relationship between the two young men has not. Jerry is as worldly-wise as ever and Alec is as naive as when the pair first met. For example, it had never occurred to Alec that Alicia could be lying when she told Alec that Frederick Moore was not his father. Jerry laughs at Alec's innocence in never having thought of such a thing and remarks wryly that despite his lack of experience Alec is 'the one they'll make an officer out of'. As the evening draws to an end and Alec becomes too drunk to make his way home alone, Jerry takes care of his more vulnerable friend by defending him against the rather derisive comments of the villagers and taking it upon himself to ensure that Alec gets home safely. They end up back at the lake, where their friendship began and, as they did when they first met, they swim together. This link to their earliest meeting and their childhood fun demonstrates that, no matter how much the world may change, the relationship between these two friends is as it always has been.

The next morning, Alec joins the army and is sent to Belfast for six weeks of training. Jerry's prediction proves correct and Alec is made an officer the moment he joins the army, while Jerry enlists as a private. The pair do not have a chance to talk to one another properly until their six weeks of training is over. As usual, Jerry is the voice of experience and the one to whom Alec turns for advice. In a reversal of what would normally be expected of a conversation between an officer and an enlisted man, it is Alec who asks Jerry if the war will end soon and what the front line will be like. They do not talk for long as

> For all that their lives have changed, the relationship between the two young men has not

Jerry is aware that their respective ranks mean they should not be seen to be friendly with one another. As Alec is the narrator, we do not learn if Jerry makes friends with his fellow soldiers, but it is reasonably safe to assume that he does. Alec, however, does not, a fact which is commented on by a disapproving Major Glendinning. Jerry is the only one with whom he seems able to let down his guard. Jerry can draw Alec out of his shell in a way nobody else seems able to do. Consequently, Alec is determined to seek out his friend whenever he gets the chance.

Like Alicia, Major Glendinning is determined to separate the young men and to make Alec live up to the expectations of his class and his position in the army

There is little doubt that this continuation of their friendship is one of the last outcomes Alicia would have predicted or wanted when she insisted that Alec fight in the war. All is not plain sailing for the friends, however, despite their being in the same regiment. Major Glendinning proves to be a ferocious antagonist in Alec and Jerry's relationship, far outstripping Alicia Moore in that he has the power of life and death over the two young men and has made it clear from the outset that he 'has no scruples about meting out the ultimate' should his orders be disobeyed. He tells Alec that he will have no fraternising between the officers and the enlisted men and he expresses his dislike and distrust of Jerry from the start. Like Alicia, Major Glendinning is determined to separate the young men and to make Alec live up to the expectations of his class and his position in the army.

Alec does not defy Major Glendinning openly but he continues to see Jerry whenever he can. The introduction of the personable, charming Bennett into Alec's life does not affect his friendship with Jerry. This is interesting as Bennett is fond of Alec and would seem to be a more suitable friend than Jerry, in the eyes of the establishment at least. However, Alec quietly but stubbornly persists in seeking Jerry out and in including him in the horse-riding excursions organised by Bennett. Major Glendinning is as unsuccessful in ending the friendship between the pair as Alicia Moore was.

Jerry notices that the conditions at the front are taking a toll on Alec's health and, even though he is just as ill and exhausted as Alec is, he tries to take care of his friend in whatever way he can. For example, he treats Alec's swollen, chilblain-covered feet and legs by rubbing rum into them. Alec, in turn, asks Jerry if his own feet are suffering but Jerry dismisses the notion, saying that he doesn't 'take these things as hard' as Alec. Such affection and consideration is all the more striking because it is set against the backdrop of a brutal, uncaring world in which men are seen as little more than cannon fodder to be sacrificed for the war effort. Alec and Jerry's relationship is the one bright light in an otherwise dark and bleak setting.

It is hardly surprising that the major should fail in his efforts to separate Alec and Jerry. Jerry is the only person with whom Alec is truly comfortable and truly happy. The relationship between the two young men is a fraternal, platonic one. With Jerry, and Jerry alone, Alec finds himself able to express his affection for another person and even become physically close to that person without any awkwardness. When other people touch Alec, there seems to be a hidden agenda. Alicia holds her son's arm or kisses him, but in an angry, controlling way. Alec says of her hands that they 'bit into [my] arm, like angry little teeth'. He shies away from contact with his mother whenever possible, finding her touch repulsive. In the same way, when Major Glendinning touches Alec's shoulder in a gesture that is meant to be somewhat kindly, Alec shudders with disgust. Bennett's gestures of affection, though different to those of Alicia or Major Glendinning, are equally unwelcome. It is only with Jerry that Alec is relaxed and comfortable. There is nothing controlling and nothing sexual in the way the pair cling to each other for warmth and comfort when Jerry returns to the farmhouse at West Outre after he has run away to search for his missing father. They are like brothers, offering one another what consolation and comfort they can.

We know from the outset that this relationship does not end happily. Alec says in the opening lines of the novel that he loves 'no living

> Jerry is the only person with whom Alec is truly comfortable and truly happy

person' and is ready to face his death without any great sadness. The tragic reason for Alec's ready acceptance of death and for his facing execution in the first place is revealed in the final section of the text. Events unfold quite rapidly, and once they are set in motion it is clear that there is no going back. Jerry receives a letter from his mother, telling him that his father is missing in action and asking him to find out what has happened. Loyally, Jerry decides to do as he is asked, even though he knows that he is unlikely to be given leave to go and find his father. He asks Alec to help him and to approach Major Glendinning on his behalf. This is significant, as Jerry has never asked anything of Alec without offering something in return. He refuses Alec's offer of financial help for the Crowe family in the same way that he refused Alec's offer of a job in the Moores' stables some time before. Jerry

> Jerry does not abuse his friendship with Alec and values the relationship too much to jeopardise it by becoming beholden to his friend

does not abuse his friendship with Alec and values the relationship too much to jeopardise it by becoming beholden to his friend. In this instance, though, he has no other option and he is not asking for himself but for his mother's sake. Major Glendinning has already made it quite clear that he dislikes Jerry and it is highly unlikely that he would give him leave if Jerry were to ask him directly.

Alec agrees to speak to the major but neither he nor Jerry is very hopeful. As might have been expected, Major Glendinning refuses the request and is angry that Alec should have approached him on Jerry's behalf. This is the first time in Alec and Jerry's relationship that Jerry has asked for Alec's help and Alec has failed him. While Jerry does not rebuke Alec in any way, the incident reinforces Alec's belief that he is useless. As he notes the following morning when he fails to secure even a brief tea break for his men, he cannot give his men 'comfort in any way'.

Jerry, having tried to get leave through the proper channels, takes matters into his own hands and goes in search of his father. He leaves without telling Alec of his intention, possibly to spare his friend from being implicated in his crime. After all, Major Glendinning has always made it clear that he will not hesitate to punish anyone who disobeys his orders or threatens the smooth running of the army. Alec is dismayed to hear of Jerry's desertion and he worries for his friend. Jerry's abrupt return one night does little to ease Alec's anxiety. Jerry is soaked and exhausted and Alec fetches him some dry clothes and a bottle of brandy. The pair lie in bed together for warmth and comfort. Jerry is more concerned for Alec than for himself and apologises for leaving without telling him. Even in his worst times, Jerry feels protective of his friend and selflessly puts Alec's feelings first. However, Jerry is at the end of his tether and admits to Alec that he is frightened and unsure of what he should do next. He asks Alec to help him and to advise him on the best course of action. This is despite Alec's complete failure to help Jerry in any practical way in the past. For only the second time in their relationship, Jerry truly needs Alec and relies on him to see him through this difficult time. His trust and hope are, unfortunately, as misplaced as they were when he asked Alec to speak to Major Glendinning about compassionate leave. Alec advises him to stay and face the music and Jerry agrees to do so. There seems to be no other realistic option. It is a testament to the strength of Alec and Jerry's relationship that Jerry turns to his friend in this moment of crisis.

> Even in his worst times, Jerry feels protective of his friend and selflessly puts Alec's feelings first

Jerry is found in Alec's room before he can go and surrender to the major. Alec tries to defend his friend against Major Glendinning but is as unsuccessful as ever. The major is determined to punish Jerry and he is as good as his word. Alec can scarcely take it in when he hears that not only is Jerry to be executed but that he, Alec, is expected to take charge of the firing squad. He is completely helpless to save his friend. What is more, the major points out that if Alec does not follow this order he will also be executed. Alec is devastated but realises that there is nothing he can do to change the major's mind on this issue. Jerry will die.

The final scene between Jerry and Alec is heartbreaking. Jerry brings up the subject of their old dream of starting a racing yard together. This dream has been Alec's refuge in difficult times but now it is Jerry who needs it. Alec takes charge, uncharacteristically. He asks Jerry to sing him a song. Jerry launches into a verse of 'The Croppy Boy' as Alec readies his revolver. He places his hand over Jerry's, Jerry looks into his eyes and, in a final act of love and mercy, Alec shoots his friend dead.

The book ends as it began. Alec sits alone in prison, awaiting execution. He faces death with equanimity as he has nothing left to live for now that Jerry is dead. Their relationship was the only thing that made his lonely life worth living. Without Jerry, he does not want to go on. This tragic end to the relationship is both bleak and oddly uplifting. On the one hand, it tells us that love and friendship are not enough and that goodness and kindness will not prevail in this world; but on the other hand it shows the triumph of loyalty and selfless love over all other concerns. Alec places his friendship with Jerry above all other things, even his own life.

Hero/Heroine/Villain

Ordinary Level

Note

In this mode, students may choose a hero **or** heroine **or** villain from their Comparative Study texts.

Past questions on this mode of comparison have tended to focus on the following:
- *Why you find the hero/heroine/villain interesting*
- *Why you consider the character to be a hero/heroine/villain*
- *What part the hero/heroine/villain plays in the storyline.*

Villain

Alicia Moore is most certainly the villain of *How Many Miles to Babylon?*. She is a self-absorbed, cruel, manipulative, cold woman. Because of her villainy, her husband's life is ruined and her son is sent to his death. If it weren't for her cruelty and selfishness, Alec would not have joined the British army.

We see Alicia's nature emerge early in the novel when she dismisses her son's piano tutor because she has taken a personal dislike to him. Her reasons are ridiculous; she says he has 'an appalling smell' and accuses him of bringing 'disease and poverty' into the house. The fact that the man will lose his job and her son will be deprived of a tutor because of her actions does not affect her decision at all. This is our first real indication that Alicia Moore is someone who puts her own happiness first, even above that of her only child.

Alicia's selfishness deprives Alec of a normal childhood. As well as dismissing the piano tutor, she refuses to allow Alec to go away to school, thereby depriving him of the chance to meet other boys of his own age. Nor does she replace this lack of company in his life with any maternal love or kindness. Alicia's only concern is that Alec should be good company for her; his needs mean nothing to her. When Alec does manage to find a friend, Jerry Crowe, Alicia puts a stop to the friendship as soon as she hears of it. Her excuse for doing so is that Jerry is of a lower social class and therefore unsuitable as a friend for Alec, but it is hard to find any justification for her decision as she offers her son no alternative to Jerry.

It might be argued that Alicia is so unhappy with her own life that she simply takes her bitterness and frustration out on those around her but that argument does not hold up when we look at her behaviour as the novel progresses. After all, Alec's father is equally unhappy and in the same loveless, dysfunctional marriage but he does not try to make his family suffer as a result of his own misery. Alicia most certainly does and, to make matters worse, she delights in it. This enjoyment of another's pain is part of what makes Alicia Moore a truly villainous woman.

> This enjoyment of another's pain is part of what makes Alicia Moore a truly villainous woman

Alicia Moore's treatment of her husband is cruel and malicious. She holds Frederick in contempt and blames him for much of her own discontent. He, for his part, gives her everything she asks for, but it is not enough. If he does what she asks, she calls him weak and ineffectual, and if he tries to stand up to her, she belittles him and insists on getting her own way. Her cruelty towards her husband is magnified by the fact that she makes no effort to hide her hatred from Alec, and the young boy is witness to his father's humiliation on a number of occasions. At Alicia's command, Frederick cautions Alec against continuing his friendship with Jerry. It is clear that Frederick's heart is not in this task but he obeys his wife's order. His words of warning are gentle, though, and Alicia is impatient with what she sees as his lack of authority. Having insisted that he speak to Alec, she now undermines what authority Frederick does possess by cutting in when he speaks and accusing him of going 'on and on about nothing'. It is clear that Frederick is upset by his wife's treatment of him (Alec notices his hand trembling as he picks up his glass) but he

THE COMPARATIVE STUDY: **HERO/HEROINE/VILLAIN**

does not defend himself, merely agreeing mildly that he is ineffective. His acquiescence seems to enrage Alicia further and she goes on to twist the knife in the wound by adding that he is not only ineffective but old as well.

It is not enough for Alicia to hate her husband; she is also determined that her son shall side with her and share her contempt for Frederick. To her annoyance, this is not the case and Frederick and Alec become closer, particularly once Alec begins to help his father with the management of the estate. This infuriates Alicia, who had envisioned Alec growing into a companion for her as he reached manhood. Because she is completely self-absorbed, she sees her son's worth as being directly linked to how useful he is to her. She does not have normal maternal love for Alec, and when she realises that he is not going to be good company for her after all, she decides to use him to hurt her husband.

The outbreak of war provides Alicia with an ideal opportunity to achieve several of her villainous goals at once. If Alec joins the army she will be able to bask in the reflected glory of his heroism. She will break her husband's heart by sending his son away, and she will punish Alec for becoming too like his father and for not growing into an adoring companion for her.

> Alicia knows Frederick's horror of losing his son in the war and she smiles maliciously when her husband reacts violently to her vocal admiration of John Redmond's call to arms

Alicia knows Frederick's horror of losing his son in the war and she smiles maliciously when her husband reacts violently to her vocal admiration of John Redmond's call to arms. Alec's father ages visibly as the war continues and his health begins to fail as worry and unhappiness take their toll. Far from treating her ageing husband with any consideration, Alicia delights in his misery.

It is the death of a local man which eventually sets the seal on Alec's fate. Alicia is thrilled by the news and seems to have no concern whatsoever for the fact that a young man has lost his life. Instead, she is delighted that she was in the dead soldier's house when the telegram arrived. Proximity to such drama delights Alicia and she looks at Alec with 'strangely excited eyes'. It is as if she sees him in the light of the war hero he might become and imagines how she would play an even larger role in the drama should a telegram arrive announcing his death. Whether or not Alicia wants Alec to be killed is debatable, but it is ominous that she should choose that evening to determine on his going to war. There is something grotesque about a mother being excited to hear about the death of a young man and, having heard the news, deciding that she will send her own son off to fight as soon as possible. Alicia Moore is revealing herself as more than just cruel and self-absorbed; she seems positively evil and a most unnatural mother.

Nothing can dissuade Alicia Moore from achieving her aim of having a serving soldier for a son. Alec and his father do not believe she means it when she broaches the subject the first time, but she is deadly serious. Typically, her way of bringing up the topic is malicious and cruel. She starts by seeming to show a solicitous interest in her husband's health, saying that he

> *'when Alexander goes to war you won't have him to rely on as you do now'*

seems to have slowed down in recent days and should perhaps see a doctor. He dismisses her apparent concern, saying mildly that he is merely old. Of course, Alicia has no interest in her husband's health and is merely setting him up for a shock. Alicia says that Frederick should get in shape because 'when Alexander goes to war you won't have him to rely on as you do now'. Alec and his father laugh and Alicia lets the matter drop until after dinner, when she repeats her assertion that Alec will join up. Alec's father begs her not to take his son away but Alicia cruelly scorns him, calling him an 'old man' and making it quite clear that, as usual, she will have her way.

Alicia's villainy might seem to have reached its zenith, but in fact she can, and does, act even more monstrously. Her husband is a spent force and his spirit is broken. Still, Alec himself may yet thwart Alicia's plans, so she goes to his room to talk to him and to ensure that he obeys her wishes. She begins by criticising Alec and his father, comparing them to one another in an unflattering manner. Again she repeats that Alec is a disappointment to her and that he has not grown into the companion she wished for. Therefore, he must please her in another way: by going to war. When Alec refuses, Alicia calls him a coward. When Alec does not react to his mother's goading, she tries another angle. She attempts to make Alec feel responsible for her unhappy life, saying that she only stayed with her husband for the sake of the child. This is almost laughable, as there has been nothing in Alicia's manner so far in the novel to suggest that she ever does anything for anyone but herself. Seeing that this approach is also failing, Alicia decides to play her trump card. In an act of cold, calculated cruelty, she tells Alec

> In an act of cold, calculated cruelty, she tells Alec that Frederick Moore is not his father

that Frederick Moore is not his father. Alec's world falls apart around his ears as he realises that his only positive family relationship is based on a lie. Alicia, for her part, dismisses Alec's horrified reaction with her customary impatience and cold detachment. She does not care how Alec feels; she is happy because she has succeeded in breaking his ties with his father, thereby ensuring that he has no reason to stay at home any longer.

It is almost impossible to imagine a mother so devoid of maternal instinct or basic human kindness that she would be willing to drive her son to near-suicidal despair in order to get her way. Yet this is exactly what Alicia Moore succeeds in doing and she shows not one iota of remorse at any time.

After this victory of villainy over kindness and love, Alicia seems content. Her husband is crushed, her son off to the front. Now Alicia can indulge her dramatic side and she is every inch the adoring mother as she says goodbye to her son the following morning. Her eyes are 'the most triumphant blue' as she exchanges final words with Alec. Her only concern is that she see him in uniform and that he write to her regularly. It would be reasonable to assume that any letters from Alec would be shown to members of Alicia's social circle, given as evidence of her son's bravery and used to show how much she was suffering as the mother of the absent young man. When Alec fails to deliver the required level of correspondence, Alicia is annoyed and writes to him to say that she is 'wounded' by his refusal to stay in touch with her. As usual, her only concern is for herself and she expresses no interest or anxiety about her son's well-being.

Our final impression of Alicia Moore is that she is an unredeemed villain: a cruel, cold, calculating, evil woman who uses others to achieve her own ends. That a mother could send her son to fight in the war simply to spite her husband and to punish both husband and son for failing her is truly monstrous. Although we never find out how the news of Alec's execution affects Frederick Moore, it is safe to say that Alec is probably right when he says that the news 'may kill him'. It is also safe to imagine that neither her son's death nor her husband's sorrow could ever touch the hard heart of Alicia Moore.

Aspects of Story: Tension, Climax or Resolution

Ordinary Level

Past questions on this mode of comparison have tended to focus on the following:

- *How does the tension, climax or resolution hold your interest in the story being told?*
- *What is the importance of the tension, climax or resolution in the text?*
- *Discuss a key moment in which the tension, climax or resolution is clearly shown.*

Tension

It might appear difficult to create tension in a novel when we know from the opening lines how the story ends, but Jennifer Johnston's masterful storytelling manages to keep the reader engrossed from the first page to the last. We are swept along in the story of Alec's tragic life, and although we know how his life will end, we wonder how he has come to this sorry pass.

The flashback technique used in *How Many Miles to Babylon?* brings us back to Alec Moore's childhood and lonely upbringing in the Big House. We empathise with the solitary, lonely little boy trapped in a dysfunctional family and deprived of the chance to meet other children of his own age. Jerry Crowe appears like a breath of fresh air, showing Alec that there is a possibility of a meaningful and happy relationship with another person. And yet, Jerry's increasing importance in Alec's life adds to the sense of tension. We know that Alec, as he faces death, claims that he 'loves no living person', so there are only two possibilities: either his friendship with Jerry comes to nothing, or else Jerry dies. Far from removing tension and suspense, our knowledge of the ending of the novel makes us wonder all the more what went wrong in Alec's life.

As Alec recalls the events that have led him to imprisonment and a death sentence, we see that both internal and external forces conspire to make his life difficult. He has to struggle against a dysfunctional family and a self-absorbed, controlling mother, and it is obvious from the start that he does not have the strength of character to stand up to the domineering Alicia Moore. Life in the Moore household is strained and tense. Alec recalls the 'comfortable meals and uncomfortable talk' in the dining room each day and the conversations between his parents which are described as being like 'some terrible game'. The image of Alec sitting at the table every day while his parents speak to each other in voices that are never raised but are always 'malevolent and cool' effectively conveys the tension and unhappiness surrounding the young boy.

Alec recalls the 'comfortable meals and uncomfortable talk' in the dining room each day and the conversations between his parents which are described as being like 'some terrible game'

Alec's friendship with Jerry brings him some much-needed happiness and normality, but it also adds to the tension in the novel. We know that Alec is a member of the Protestant Ascendancy and as such is unlikely to be permitted a close relationship with a Catholic boy from the peasant class. Alec's delight at finding a friend is touching, but from the start we are aware that the boys must keep their relationship a secret. Alec knows that he can never visit Jerry's house, nor can Jerry visit his. Society in general, and the boys' families in particular, would frown on their association. We wonder whether the pair will succeed in keeping their friendship under wraps or whether they will be discovered. Our sympathies are more with Alec than with Jerry in this case. Alec's lonely, friendless life is changed and brightened by Jerry Crowe's friendship, and we know that if that connection is removed, Alec will be forced to retreat to the hostile, bitter environment that is his home life.

Pressure mounts on the young men's relationship as they grow older. Their lives take different paths; Jerry has to leave school and get a job to support his family while Alec's life remains largely unchanged. We wonder if their friendship will continue or will they be driven apart by the fact that they have less and less in common as they leave their childhoods behind.

Inevitably, the friendship is discovered and Alec's parents endeavour to put a stop to what they view as an 'unsuitable relationship'. Alicia in particular is a powerful antagonistic force and we wonder if she will succeed in permanently separating the friends. To an extent, Alicia does succeed in that she takes Alec away to Europe for four months. When he returns, he begins to work with his father on estate business and we wonder if he is finally embracing the values of his class and accepting the differences between himself and his childhood friend. He returns to Wicklow in the autumn but does not see Jerry at close quarters for several months.

> we wonder if the pair will survive, let alone manage to sustain their relationship now that they are separated by rank as well as by social class

The tension created by Alec's separation from Jerry is eased somewhat when he finally meets Jerry at the point-to-point the following spring. Alec is as pleased as ever to see his old friend and after a brief period of awkwardness they fall into easy conversation again. Jerry's initial reluctance to chat to Alec is overcome by Alec's enthusiastic and open manner as he praises Jerry's horse. However, Alicia soon intervenes and we wonder once more if her determination to keep Alec away from Jerry is stronger than Alec's determination to remain friendly with his childhood companion.

The introduction of the war in Europe adds greatly to the tension in the novel. The story moves to the battlefields of Flanders and the suspense mounts as we wonder if the pair will survive, let alone manage to sustain their relationship, now that they are separated by rank as well as by social class.

Life at the front is fraught with danger and Alec and Jerry's friendship is threatened not only by the threat of one or both of them losing their life to enemy fire but also by the hostility and disapproval of Major Glendinning. The major is more determined than Alicia

Moore when it comes to keeping the pair apart and his repeated threats that he will have no hesitation in 'meting out the ultimate' to anyone who disobeys him adds to the tension of the text. We hope that neither Jerry nor Alec will incur the major's wrath but at the same time we suspect that such an outcome may be inevitable. The opening lines of the novel come back to haunt us and the tension is increased as we reflect on Alec's remark about loving 'no living person'. Now we feel that the most reasonable interpretation of this comment is that Jerry dies before the end of the novel and we wonder how such a thing could come about. Will he be killed in battle? Such an outcome would hardly be surprising but it still does not explain Alec's impending execution.

Jerry's letter from home precipitates the chain of events that leads to the tragic ending of the novel. For the first time, Jerry needs Alec's help and Alec is unable to do anything for him. He agrees to ask the major if he will grant Jerry compassionate leave to search for his father but he admits himself that his voice doesn't 'sound exactly hopeful' and we sense that it is unlikely he will be able to achieve much on Jerry's behalf. Major Glendinning has made it clear that he disapproves of Alec's friendship with Jerry and this disapproval radiates from him when Alec makes his request. It is not surprising that the major refuses to allow Jerry any leave but we wonder how Jerry will react to such news. He has never shown any great respect for rules and regulations.

'each new death was another barrier down, another step in one's own direction'

We share Alec's relief when he sees Jerry at Stand To the following morning. This relief is short-lived, however, as Jerry disappears. The fighting at the front is fierce and Alec has no time to dwell on the fact that he hasn't seen Jerry. The escalation of the fighting at this point in the novel foreshadows the violence that is to come. Alec says that the men have little room left in their hearts for pity at this stage, so numbed and sickened are they by all the slaughter they have seen. Alec says that 'each new death was another barrier down, another step in one's own direction'.

It is only when he gets back to the farmhouse at West Outre that Alec realises Jerry must have gone absent without leave. Knowing that Major Glendinning will not hesitate to punish Jerry severely for desertion, Alec is horrified and we share his dismay as he wonders what Jerry was hoping to achieve by taking matters into his own hands.

Climax

The highest point of tension in the novel occurs when Jerry returns from his search for his father. His decision to come back is shocking and unexpected, particularly as he must know that he will face a court martial on charges of desertion in the face of the enemy. The fact that he left from the front at a time of exceptionally heavy fighting means that he will almost certainly be found guilty. Again, Major Glendinning's warnings about 'meting out the ultimate' come to mind.

Jerry is exhausted and soaking wet when he arrives into Alec's bedroom. Alec does his best to help his friend in a practical way by fetching him some dry clothes and lying beside him in the bed in the hope that his body heat will warm Jerry. This is a touching scene but we know that Alec can do little more than this for his friend. The farm is filled with soldiers and the chances of Jerry escaping are virtually non-existent. There are constant reminders of the threat of discovery. As Alec and Jerry talk, the noise from downstairs adds to the tension by emphasising how close the other men are. It seems almost inevitable that Jerry will be found and arrested. Jerry himself seems aware of this and tells Alec that he knows of 'no hole to hide in round here that I wouldn't be blown out of by one side or the other'. At that moment, there is a burst of sudden laughter from the floor below. The timing makes it seem as if someone is mocking Jerry's predicament. Although it may only be someone laughing in his sleep, the laughter seems grotesque under the circumstances and reinforces Jerry's remark that his own side is as likely to wish him harm as the Germans.

> The farm is filled with soldiers and the chances of Jerry escaping are virtually non-existent. There are constant reminders of the threat of discovery

The situation seems hopeless and Alec watches helplessly as Jerry takes the brandy bottle and quickly drinks himself into insensibility. The drink affects him quickly, no doubt due to his weakened physical condition. In a shockingly sudden and unexpected movement, Jerry hurls the empty bottle across the room and it shatters against the wall with 'an explosion of sound'. The word 'explosion' reminds us of the shelling and death at the front line and of Jerry's words about being 'blown out of' any possible refuge by his own side if not by the enemy. There is little hope of escape. The farmhouse, which had been a refuge of sorts, is now as dangerous as the front line.

Jerry falls into sleep or unconsciousness and Alec is paralysed with horror and fear as he realises that the noise has alerted the men downstairs. The situation is as tense as if the footsteps he hears coming up the stairs were those of enemy soldiers.

We have a brief moment of hope when the first person to arrive in the room is the sympathetic and kindly O'Keefe. He is unsure what to do for the best but, realising that Alec is unequal to the situation, he offers to take over. He advises Alec to leave so as not to be accused of 'aiding and abetting' Jerry.

Any hope we may have had that the situation might end well is dashed when the door opens and Sergeant Barry enters. The sergeant has always disliked both Jerry and Alec and he wastes no time in calling for his men to come and arrest Jerry. His contempt for Alec is shown by his refusal to salute him, which adds to the impression of Alec's lack of authority and power in this situation. The chances of his being able to speak convincingly to Major Glendinning on his friend's behalf seem remote indeed if even the sergeant is unimpressed by him. The semi-conscious Jerry is dragged away and Alec can only watch helplessly.

Events continue to unfold with horrifying speed. A shocked and dazed Alec is summoned to appear before Major Glendinning to discuss Jerry's reappearance. The major is angry at the circumstances in which Jerry was found and asks Alec if he realises that he is fighting in a war. His question: 'Do you realise what you are wearing?' seems to push Alec to the limit. He replies that he thinks the uniform is 'some sort of fancy dress' and this, in turn, pushes the major to the limit of his patience. He strikes Alec a ferocious blow across the face with his cane. That the major should lose his self-control in this way and that he should act with such sudden savagery indicates that everything is falling apart and that the violence of war has now reached far beyond the front lines.

The extent of the crisis is made clear the following day when Major Glendinning tells Alec that not only is Jerry sentenced to death but he, Alec, is to command the firing squad. This horrific prospect appalls Alec but the major tells him he has no option. If he refuses, he will be shot too and someone else will take charge of Jerry's execution. On hearing this, Alec appears to give up hope. Major Glendinning is pleased, believing he has succeeded in making Alec see sense at last.

Resolution

How Many Miles to Babylon? opens with Alec in his prison cell, awaiting execution, and it ends the same way. The reader knows how the story will end but, even so, the tragedy is no less shocking and heartbreaking when it does occur.

At the end of the novel, Jerry and Alec have been pushed to a place from which there is no return. Their whole lives seem to have been spent trying to escape, trying to find a better life and trying to remain friends despite the forces threatening their relationship. They have each joined the army for different reasons but neither joined because they wanted to. Alec says at the start of the book that he is 'committed to no cause' and loves 'no living person'. Jerry is equally uncommitted to the war effort. It seems ironic that both men should lose their lives because of a war in which they have no interest and no emotional involvement.

The ending of *How Many Miles to Babylon?* is bleak and hopeless. Alec, faced with the certain death of his only friend, sees no point in living and makes the fatal decision to end Jerry's life himself. This is an act of mercy akin to Major Glendinning's ending the life of the injured soldier in No Man's Land, although it is unlikely that the major would view it that way. Unwittingly, however, Major Glendinning is responsible for Alec's final act of courage and love. It is the major who tells Alec that there is no hope whatsoever for Jerry. He also advises Alec to ensure that the men in the firing squad 'shoot straight' so that Jerry dies as quickly as possible. Alec listens to this advice and the major believes that he has finally seen sense and accepted the inevitable. What he does not know, of course, is that his words have in fact made Alec determined to be the one to ensure that Jerry dies quickly and thus does not have to spend the night in mental torment.

Jerry and Alec's final moments together are spent trying to think of happier times and regretting the fact that they never got to become partners in the racing yard of their dreams. Alec pretends that he will go ahead with the yard although he knows quite well that he is about to end Jerry's life and in so doing will effectively end his own life, too. The major has told him plainly that if he does anything to interfere with Jerry's execution he will be shot and his body sent home to his parents.

The novel ends abruptly. Alec encourages Jerry to sing a song and when Jerry breaks into his old favourite, 'The Croppy Boy', Alec readies his revolver. Jerry is aware of Alec's intentions and his eyes fill with tears, but he silently gives Alec his consent by holding Alec's hand tightly and smiling at his old friend as Alec pulls the trigger. Jerry's hand slips slowly out of Alec's grasp as his body slides to the floor. Alec stands still with his eyes shut, awaiting arrest.

> he silently gives Alec his consent by holding Alec's hand tightly and smiling at his old friend as Alec pulls the trigger

The feeling we are left with at the end of this novel is one of deep sorrow at the waste of two lives. At the same time, there is something positive and moving about Alec's selflessness and loyalty. He has shown courage and decisiveness as his mother and Major Glendinning wished him to do. However, he has not chosen to comply with their wishes but has instead used his new-found resolve to spare his friend the horror of death by firing squad. Alec is at last a hero. The tragedy is that his heroism costs him his life.

glossary

· ·

Note

The words in this glossary are only explained in the context in which they appear in this book. Fuller definitions and examples of other usages can be found in any good dictionary.

Acquiescence: agreement

Albeit: although

Cloistered: separated or sheltered from the outside world

Colloquialism: informal language used in speech

Curate: a low-ranking clergyman

Devoid: lacking in something

Dissipate: to drive something away or make it disappear

Enigma: one who is mysterious or hard to understand

Equanimity: calm self-control in the face of a very difficult or stressful situation

Flout: to disobey a law or a rule deliberately

Forgo: do without something pleasant

Frivolous: behaving in a silly or light-hearted way when the situation demands that you should be serious

Incongruity: not in keeping/incompatible

Ineffectual: weak or incapable of producing results

Obtuse: not thinking clearly or intelligently

Point-to-point: a cross-country horse race over fences and other obstacles

Pragmatic: practical and willing to look at the situation as it really is rather than the way you would like it to be

Social mores:	the customs, habits and manners of a particular group in society
Solicitous:	helpful/showing care or concern
Stultifyingly:	in a tedious, restrictive or repetitive manner
Superficial:	trivial, shallow, insubstantial
Subjugate:	to bring under control in a way which allows no freedom
Thwart:	to prevent someone from doing something
Zenith:	the peak or the highest point